BE SONS OF YOUR FATHER
Insights into the Sermon on the Mount

OTHER BOOKS BY PETER J. RIGA

The Church of the Poor
The Church and Revolution
The Church Made Relevant
The Church Renewed
John XXIII and the City of Man
Sin and Penance
Peace on Earth
Catholic Thought in Crisis
Student Guide to Pacem in Terris
New Horizons for the People of God

alba house   **alba house** DIVISION OF THE SOCIETY OF ST. PAUL   STATEN ISLAND, N.Y. 10314

BE
SONS
OF YOUR
FATHER

PETER J. RIGA

Nihil Obstat:
    Gall Higgins, O.F.M. Cap.
    Censor Librorum

Imprimatur:
    Joseph P. O'Brien, S.T.D.
    Vicar General, New York, N.Y. — February 27, 1969

226.9

Library of Congress Catalog Card Number: 75-77648

Designed, printed and bound in the U.S.A. by the Pauline Fathers and Brothers of the Society of St. Paul at Staten Island, New York as a part of their communications apostolate.

DEDICATION

For the many innocent victims of the war in Vietnam.

Blessed are those who mourn, for they shall be comforted (Mt. 5:4).

CONTENTS

PREFACE

The following pages are nothing more than a simple attempt to explain that which constitutes the central core of the life and moral activity of the follower of Christ. It seems that a small book which would give such an explanation without cumbersome apparatus of footnotes and bibliography, would be, if nothing else, a small contribution in the essential task of understanding the Word of God. That is why Vatican II stressed this reading, contemplating and activating of the written Word of God:

> The Church has always venerated the divine Scriptures just as she venerates the Body of the Lord, since from the table of both the Word of God and the Body of Christ she unceasingly receives and offers to the faithful the bread of life, especially in the sacred liturgy. She has always regarded the Scriptures together with sacred tradition as the supreme role of faith, and will ever do so. For, inspired by God and committed once and for all to writing, they impart the Word of God himself without change, and make the voice of the Holy Spirit resound in the words of the prophets and apostles. Therefore, like the Christian religion itself, all the preaching of the Church must be nourished and ruled by Sacred Scripture. For in the sacred books, the Father, who is in Heaven, meets his children with great love and speaks with them; and the force and power in the Word of God is so great that it remains the support and energy

of the Church, the pure and perennial source of spiritual life (*Constitution on Revelation,* Art. 21).

It is my modest hope that the following small work will introduce some into the beauty and power of this Word of God.

I would like to thank Thomas Nelson and Sons for permission to quote from *The Holy Bible*: *Revised Standard Version* (1957).

Peter J. Riga

St. Mary's College, California
November 1, 1968

INTRODUCTION

THE SERMON ON THE MOUNT
Mt. 5:1-48; 6:1-34; 7:1-28

The account of the Sermon on the Mount in St. Matthew is one of the longest accounts of the whole first gospel. It is composed of three chapters or about 107 verses. It seems to have been more or less artificially composed to meet the needs of various themes which run throughout the text of the gospel. This sermon is not found as such in Mark's gospel, and the narrative of Luke (6:17-49) seems to have dropped most of what is conserved in the account of Matthew. This introduces us to the first problem of the Sermon — the composition of the text.

The Sermon is a composition of typical sayings ("logia") of Jesus collected here by the evangelists around various themes. We may say, moreover, that everything contained in the narrative of St. Luke is contained in the narrative of St. Matthew with but three exceptions which are as follows:

(a) There is a small parable in *Lk.* 6:45 concerning a man and his treasure. It concludes with: "The good man out of the good treasure of his heart produces good; and the evil man out of his evil treasure produces evil; for out of the abundance of the heart his mouth speaks." This adage establishes the link between the heart of a man and his external actions. This is a Hebrewism; for the ancients, words are intimately related to actions since they have a power of action. If a man's heart or intention is good, so too will his actions be good, since the word is a *sign* of the actions of the heart.

(b) The text of Luke in 6:38ᵃ has: "give, and it will be given to you"— which is substantially that contained in the account of Matthew. Luke then adds a further precision to this thought: "good measure, pressed down, shaken together, running over will be put into your lap." This is nothing more than local color, for the harvesters of the time were paid at the end of the day by opening their mantels, getting all the pleats out (to make them as big as possible) and had them filled with whatever they were harvesting. The moral is that the Lord of the harvest will be as generous as possible to each person — which really adds nothing new to the basic thought of the passage.

(c) In *Lk.* 6:39 the author characterizes the literary form of the whole narrative by calling it a "parable" (cf. *Mt.* 15:15).

We may conclude that, in general, Luke is acquainted with the texts of Matthew's Sermon but prefers to include them later in his account where Christ speaks more to his disciples than to the crowd in order to complete their formation (that is, after the ninth chapter of Luke). For example:

Mt. 5:13 is found in *Lk.* 14:34-35 (Salt);
Mt. 5:25-26 appears in *Lk.* 12:58-59 (Judgment);
Mt. 6:9-13 is found in *Lk.* 11:2-4 (Our Father);
Mt. 6:19-24 is seen in *Lk.* 12:33-34 (Treasure);
Mt. 6:33 in *Lk.* 18:29-30 (Justice);
Mt. 7:12 in *Lk.* 13:23-24 (Golden Rule).

Thus, many of themes of the Sermon are contained in both gospels, but because of the different objectives of the evangelists we find them arranged differently in both accounts. Many scholars are agreed that both evangelists derived their accounts from an independent third source, but we do not wish to go into this rather complicated question at this point. Suffice it to say that for his own pedagogical reasons, Luke broke up the Sermon into the various parts of his gospel, while Matthew, who had a tendency to group like things together, put the elements of the Sermon into one section (our present narration) with little concern about chronology. For instance, Matthew places the *Our Father* immediately after the section on prayer (*Mt.* 6:7-13), which seems somewhat artificial. Such a rich prayer presupposes a certain initiation into prayer which cannot be given, as does Matthew, in the midst of one long discourse. Luke's narration (11:2-4) of the *Our Father* is much better situated within the context of fraternal charity (10:25-37) and the need of prayer and contemplation (10:38-42).

Let us first examine the passages of the "beatitudes" in Luke (6:20) and Matthew (5:1-12).

Matthew's account has Christ mounting a hill, sitting down, opening his mouth to utter the beatitudes at the very beginning of the Sermon. The crowds remain on the plain while Christ, with his disciples, are at a distance from them. It seems that the discourse is directed primarily to the disciples and only incidentally to the crowds. It is these disciples who will collect the Master's sayings and assemble them to-

gether. The mountain is mentioned since it is a parallel
to the original mountain of Mt. Sinai where the first
law (a fundamental theme of the Sermon) was given
to the chosen people who also remained at the foot
of the mountain. Christ is here represented as the
new Moses who gives the perfect law of the gospel
(fraternal love). Christ teaches the disciples so that
in their turn they might be the witnesses of his
good news to the people. They were the ones who
were to transmit this message. The "crowds" are not
only Jews but also people from Syria and the sur-
rounding regions (*Mt.* 4:25) which, presumably,
includes pagans. Thus the future universal nature of
the missionary vocation of the disciples to all peoples
is here implied. Through the disciples, Christ addresses
himself to the whole world.

In the account of Luke we also find the calling
of the original twelve for the same theological reason
as that of Matthew, but Luke is more specific than is
Matthew. Luke mentions "the twelve" and not simply
"the disciples." The "twelve" are a sort of *collegium*
associated with Jesus in his work (6:12-18). The narration of Luke begins with an all night prayer after
which Jesus chooses his Apostles. It is this small group
of men who are known technically in the New Testament as "the twelve" and who are to be the official
witnesses of Jesus after the Ascension. They are the
guarantors of the good news of salvation within the
community (cf. *Acts* 4:32-33; 15:5-24), and their witness is fundamental for the whole gospel of Luke.

Perhaps a small addition in *Lk.* 6:17 is of note:
"and he came down with them and stood on a level

place." Christ does not go up with the disciples, but he does descend to join his disciples.

We may conclude the following from both accounts of Matthew and Luke:

In Matthew, the word "crowds" is used along with "disciples" but these latter are set apart from the crowd. Christ sits down and he teaches in the custom of Hebrew rabbis. The teaching is first of all directed to his disciples and through them to the crowds (*Mt.* 5:15-16). Even in the entourage of "the disciples," the term is broader than simply "the twelve" or "the Apostles." "Disciples" here designates all who have begun to respond to the good news or who have already made their decision for Christ.

The account of Luke is somewhat different. Christ teaches the whole crowd surrounded by his disciples ("the twelve"). Christ then descends to the crowd (surrounded by the disciples). The twelve as a group are taught and formed by Christ to announce the good news to the whole world.

I
THE BEATITUDES

Before we proceed to an explanation of the beatitudes themselves, it would perhaps be profitable to
examine the literary form of this literature. The literary
form of beatitudes was originally found in the literature of the Old Testament, composed of two sections:

(a) Those who do such a thing or have such an
attitude, then

(b) They will receive such a reward or punishment
or will be in such a state or condition.

This is a basic form in the Old Testament as witness
the following psalm (*Ps.* 1):

Blessed is the man
    who walks not in the counsel of the wicked,
nor stands in the way of sinners,
nor sits in the seat of scoffers;
but his delight is in the law of the Lord,
    and on his law he meditates day and night.
He is like a tree
    planted by streams of water,

That yields its fruit in its season,
    and its leaf does not wither.
In all that he does, he prospers.

We have a perfect example of a "macharism" (blessed)
or happiness to the man who does good. On the other
hand, the one who does evil is cursed. As the second
part of this same psalm puts it:

The wicked are not so,
    but are like chaff which the wind
        drives away.
Therefore the wicked will not stand
    in judgment,
        nor sinners in the congregation of the
            righteous;
for the Lord knows the way of the righteous,
    but the way of the wicked will perish.

This same blessing or curse is transmitted by the
blessing or curse of a Patriarch, as when Jacob blessed
Isaac (*Gen.* 27:27-30). The words have an almost
independent effect in producing what they signify.
They are words of power and efficacy, appeal and
encouragement. The blessing or the curse is usually
dependent upon some condition which must be fulfilled in order to obtain the said curse or blessing.
When Luke (6:24) says: "Woe to you that are rich,
for you have received your consolation"— the curse,
of course, is dependent upon condition that the rich
continue to be greedy and selfish. Implicit in the condemnation is a certain appeal to penance, since there is

as yet some time left before the fateful hour comes, after which there can be no repentance. So too with regard to the blessing: he will continue to be blessed as long as he continues to be meek, patient, merciful, etc. Hence, we may say that one aspect of this literary form is called *kerygmatic* (proclamation in words of power of a state to be realized) in function of the other aspect, the *exhortative*, which fixes the conditions necessary for realizing that state.

This literary form appears quite frequently in the *Wisdom* literature of the Old Testament, since it was essentially geared to the training of youth or the art of living well based on the experience of the older generation (cf. *Proverbs* 3:13; 8:32; 20:7; 28:14 and in *Sirach* 1:13; 26; 2:12-14; 4:12-13; 6:32; etc.). The *Psalms* are also of this literary form (cf. 1:1-12; 32:1). The literary form of the Sermon which is found in Luke and Matthew can be seen in this Old Testament literature.

The styles of Matthew and Luke are quite different. Both give us the same number of beatitudes (8) but arrange them differently. Luke gives us four beatitudes and four corresponding curses. For example:

Lk. 6:20: "Happy are *you*, the poor, for the Kingdom of God is yours." The second person plural is used in all four of his beatitudes and curses.

Mt. 5:3: "Happy are the poor in *spirit*, for the Kingdom of heaven is theirs." In contrast to Luke, Matthew always uses the third person plural in his beatitudes and adds "of heaven" to the word "Kingdom."

Lk. 6:21: "Happy are you who cry *now*, for you

will laugh." Luke uses the word "now" (*nun*) to accentuate the difference of time: "now — then." The "now" refers to the present world under the domination of the forces of evil which is distinguished from future time, eschatological time, the Kingdom to come where all things will be put aright.

Mt. 5:4 is contradistinguished from the text of Luke: "Blessed are those who mourn, for they shall be comforted"— with no reference to a time element. It is not known whether Matthew envisioned a now or an eschatological perspective. This phenomenon, however, is present in *Lk.* 6:21: "Blessed are you who hunger now, for you shall be filled," as contrasted with *Mt.* 5:6: "Happy are those who hunger and thirst after justice, for they shall be satisfied," where we have a certain spiritualization of the notion of hunger. Luke remains on the more material plane where actual and material poverty are stressed.

It is interesting to note that in these nuances between Luke and Matthew we see clearly that Luke has not yet realized that eschatological times have already begun and that the epoc of the *parousia* has now begun. For Luke, the Kingdom is still expected to come. It is for this reason that Luke contrasts the present with future eschatology. Until now, the just have been oppressed but in the future Kingdom this situation will be set aright. As a reward, Luke promises the Kingdom to these just men.

The attitude of Matthew is quite different since his account stresses the *now* and not only the future, since the eschatological times have already begun here below in time. The Kingdom has imperfectly but really appeared in time; it is here now. The Sermon is a new style of life — it goes beyond the decalogue — of the Christian who has begun to live within eschatological time.

The composition of the beatitudes can be divided into three main categories: The beatitudes of the poor, the beatitudes of the persecuted, and the beatitudes of fraternal charity. Let us examine each of these categories.

I. *The Beatitudes of the Poor*

These are three in number and indicate to us what *kind* of Kingdom has arrived. Thus, the Kingdom has in fact arrived and, consequently, we must live according to its nature. Those who are called to this Kingdom must live in a special way, different from those who live "in the world." These "poor men" who are Christians have further obligations as listed in *Mt.* 7:1-12: They must be merciful, peacemakers, pure of heart.

In Luke, Christ addresses himself first of all to the poor, and it is this state of poverty which is necessary for obtaining a place in the Kingdom. This condition is not purely a material or sociological poverty, but it implies this condition, since Luke places heavy accent on the materiality of this condition. He is above all the evangelist of the poor (we also note the communitarian sharing of goods of the Christian community at Jerusalem in *Acts* 4:34-37). Behind this solicitude is perhaps an attempt to answer a difficulty which arose in the Roman world: most of the converts to Christianity were poor and uneducated, the "little ones" of this world. Luke attempts to answer this perplexing question.

II. *The Beatitudes of the Persecuted*

These beatitudes seem to have been composed after those concerning the poor, but scholarship is not certain whether they were composed during the lifetime of Jesus. If anything, these beatitudes of persecution date from at least the second half of the life of Jesus when he encounters persecution and opposition. This was in strong relation to the fate of the Apostles who also endured opposition and persecution almost from the beginning of their apostolate.

III. *The Beatitudes of Fraternal Charity*

These concern the peacemakers, the merciful, and in literary style are similar to the beatitudes of the poor.

We are now in a position to explain each of the beatitudes in detail.

First Beatitude: "Blessed are the poor in spirit for theirs is the Kingdom of Heaven" (Mt. 5:3).

Cf. *Lk.* 6:20[b]: "Blessed are you poor, for yours is the Kingdom of God."

One of the main characteristics of the presence of the Kingdom is that the good news of salvation is announced to the poor (*Isaiah* 61:1-8). Parallel texts can be found in *Mt.* 11:5 and *Lk.* 9:59-61. When the disciples of the Baptist come to ask Christ whether he was the expected Messiah, Christ answers by saying, among other things, that the poor have the gospel preached to them, since this is one of the principal signs that the Kingdom of God has arrived on earth. The "dead" referred to in *Mt.* 11:5 is nothing more than the spiritually weak who are to be strengthened and encouraged by the good news of salvation (cf. *Lk.* 9:59-60). All this is done in order to avoid the scandal which would naturally come at seeing a simple rabbi (Christ) establish the Kingdom. Christ gives them the proof of its establishment — the good news to the dead, the poor, etc.— and lets these disciples of John draw their own conclusions.

The biblical attitude toward the poor is remarkable in that they are held in great esteem, while in other pagan literature, they are despised or not mentioned. The *Illiad* of Homer, for instance, makes much of the aristocrats but says almost nothing about the poor and the miserable. As a matter of fact, ancient civilizations boasted about the fact that they were the descendants of the union of various gods and were all the more solicitous to avoid praising the poor and miserable in their midst.

Such was not the case with Israel mostly because, throughout her history, she had been more or less a poor nation, persecuted by the other nations. The poor, then, had a place of honor among the chosen people. Israel, as a people, always remained sensitive to misery and suffering, solicitous for the poor in their midst.

The vocabulary used to describe the poor in Israel was indicative in this regard. The Hebrew words meaning poverty or the poor are:

Rash: This is the participle of the verb "to be in want," to be without money or goods in a social sense. This word is often found in the *Wisdom* literature of the Bible, where it is used in a pejorative sense to describe a poor man who is lazy and is thus poor because of his own fault. This word, however, is *never* used by the prophets. This is noteworthy.

Dal: This word means "he who is thin" as distinguished from the rich man who is fat.

Ebron: This term dates from the time of the kings in the 9th century B.C. and is at the origin of property. The word means "he who looks with envy" as of one who has no property to one who has.

Ani: Literally means "he who serves" and is used in more of a moral sense of one who is in the continuous service of another man as distinguished from one who has power and directs others.

Anawim: The term refers to the humble, the "little ones" of the earth or the miserable and downtrodden.

The Poor in the Old Testament

There are two main sections in the Old Testament where these words are used: the Torah and the prophets. See, for example, *Ex.* 23:6,9 (the Code of the Alliance, *Exodus,* Chs. 20-23).

But the ones who most used this vocabulary were the prophets of Israel. *Amos* has an invective against the rich in 2:6:

Thus says the Lord:
> For three transgressions of Israel,
> and for four, I will not revoke the
> punishment;

because they sell the righteous for silver
> and the needy for a pair of shoes.

They that trample the head of the poor
> into the dust of the earth,

and turn aside the way of the afflicted.

The hunger of the rich for possessions and material goods led them to exploit the poor. The objective of *Amos* is to denounce the very existence of poverty among the chosen people in the face of glaring inequalities between rich and poor. The reason for this is that this social condition was an implicit denial of the solidarity of the chosen people, a denial of the fraternity in the unique salvific act of Yahweh, the God of Israel.

Isaiah attributes to the rich an attitude of pride and of self-sufficiency based on their power and wealth. This will separate them from God (cf. 2:6-12 and 5:8-16). They are independent of God and feel little need to have recourse to him in faith and trust. The danger of riches for *Isaiah* was that it makes man proudly self-sufficient. The man who possesses much cares little about the coming future of God's intervention in history.

Zephaniah had perhaps the most nuanced attitude toward poverty and insisted on a spiritual poverty. He does not approve of the exploitation of the poor by the rich. On the "day of Yahweh," Israel will be purged and only a remnant ("anawim") will be saved:

> For I will leave in the midst of you
>> a people humble and lowly ('dal' and 'ani')
> They shall seek refuge in the name
>> of the Lord,
> Those who are left in Israel ... (3:12).

The rich and the proud will be eliminated on that day of Yahweh. His teaching on poverty, however, is more nuanced than in *Isaiah*. *Zephaniah* sees a possibility of a certain spiritual poverty alongside of material poverty, which can also lead to confidence and fidelity to God. This spiritual poverty is an attitude of humility. This humility has as its characteristic to be a "little one," one who does not do what he wants but rather one who does the wishes of another. They are always at the beck and call of another — in this case, God. This is the true Israel, the remnant, which will remain after the purification of the people. They will be characterized as poor and humble, seeking refuge in God, not in their riches or military forces. This humility and poverty will be the mark of their living relationship with God. They will not be proud but faithful to the law. They are men of prayer, and that is why we can see them in many of the psalms which are mostly the prayers of these *anawim* of Israel. This is clearly seen in such psalms as Psalm 34:

> I will bless the Lord at all times;
>> his praise shall be continually in my mouth.

My soul makes its boast in the Lord;
Let the afflicted hear and be glad.
The poor man cried, and the Lord heard him,
and saved him out of all his troubles.

Here we see the theme of *joy* of the poor man in his afflictions, for he knows that it is God who strengthens and delivers him. He has absolute trust and confidence in God who does not abandon the poor but listens to them and saves them. He hears their voice and is close to those with broken hearts. Thus the poor man lives a life of living faith in Yahweh, and his hope is in God in the midst of his trials and suffering.

The Poor in the New Testament

Like the Old Testament, the New Testament gives an important place to the poor. In the time of Christ, there were diverse classes into which the poor were divided.

1. There were the sick and those who were ill: the blind, deaf, lepers, etc. It must be remembered that in those days there was little social organization, and the poor ill were on the fringes of society, eking out a living by begging and other servile activities. This reduced the ill to a deplorable state of existence. These crowds are in evidence throughout the gospels and Christ associates with them more than with any other group. The miracles of Christ are mostly performed on them as not only acts of sign value of the presence of the Kingdom but simply as acts of charity for the poor and destitute.

2. Children were also considered to belong to this group of the poor in Israel where there was a certain mystique concerning children. Children had no rights, since it was other people — adults — who made decisions for them: thus the humility of a child who obeyed the orders of another. Yet, childhood was also a time of great desires; the child makes his wants known by crying out for attention. Thus, Jesus holds up children as models to be imitated in that attitude of humility and expectation before God. Men must become like little children before they can enter into the Kingdom.

3. The third class of the poor were the public sinners or the publicly humiliated ones of society. They were the "impure" ones of Jewish law, and to be seen in their company was to be considered as impure as well. Thus, publicans, prostitutes and certain professions such as shepherds were legally unclean. Christ in the gospels is often seen in their company, and this is one of the major criticisms of the life of Jesus by the Pharisees.

In the Old Testament, money and wealth in the hands of the rich are the source of their pride, corruption and the instrument of their wicked power over other men. *Isaiah* pointed out that riches are an obstacle to the life of faith. *Zephaniah* — while he did not make a virtue of material power as such — gives us this essential teaching: those who are deprived of material goods, power, prestige, etc., confide themselves more easily to God, trust him completely. The poor man in his distress gives himself completely to God. Thus his fundamental teaching is a certain "spiritual poverty," that is, that in all things, absolute confidence and trust in God alone is a prerequisite to salvation and entrance into the Kingdom.

In the New Testament, Christ comes especially to the poor and destitute and other groups scorned by the "respectable" people of Judaism. In this sense, Christianity is opposed to all sects, to the "pure" ones. Hence, a community of the "pure" such as Qumran would have been utterly foreign to the thought and teachings of Jesus. Christ did not come to an "elite," but to all those who were despised but yet believed.

We are now in a position to understand the words of Matthew: "Blessed are the poor in spirit, for theirs is the Kingdom of Heaven" (5:3). Matthew adds the word "spirit" in order to underline the fact that true poverty is rooted in a man's heart and mind, not necessarily in a lack of material goods (*Zephaniah*). Man must surrender himself completely to God, trust him without measure. Luke (6:20) does not have this addition because throughout his gospel he glorifies material poverty. For Luke, poverty of goods is an ideal of the whole Christian community which was initially begun at Jerusalem (*Acts* 4:15). In reality, this early economic organization of the Christian community at Jerusalem became a failure, since we see St. Paul making an appeal for it to the Church at Corinth (I *Cor.* 16:1-4). Luke writes a sort of apology for this initial effort in his gospel. Most commentators argue that Luke probably was closer to the material words of Christ. Matthew, however, was more faithful to his basic teaching in this matter.

❋　❋　❋

The second beatitude concerns those who weep:

Blessed are those who mourn, for they shall be comforted (*Mt.* 5:4).

This is certainly not a reference to those who weep for sentimental reasons, but refers to all those who are tried and tested by life's difficulties and pains. Those who patiently suffer in misery and tears will be consoled. At the very heart of their suffering, God will come to fill up their desolation and emptiness. The gospel of Luke (6:2) puts this consolation in eschatological prespective: those who mourn now will be consoled on the last day.

❊   ❊   ❊

Blessed are the meek, for they shall inherit the earth (*Mt.* 5:5).

The word "meek" in the Bible refers to one who is humble, who does not menace others when he is hurt and despised, and who, in reality, is non-violent toward others. In *Mt.* 21:5 we have the same word applied to Jesus himself: "Behold your King is coming to you, humble (meek) and mounted on an ass." The relationship between "meekness" and the "ass" is significant since this was the animal which signified peace and non-violence, as opposed to a horse which was an animal of war and worldly power (cf. *Zechariah* 9:9). Jesus is humble or meek, and the sign of this is that he rides an ass in his triumphal entry into Jerusalem. His triumph is not by worldly power or force, but by love, obedience and humility.

This same word appears again in *Mt.* 11:28-30:

Come to me, all who labor and are heavyladen, and I will give you rest. Take my yoke upon you, and learn from me; for I am gentle (meek) and lowly (humble) of heart, and you will find rest for your souls.

The image of the yoke is that of animals — a wooden bar which rests on the neck of the animal in order to pull a cart or wagon. To be under a "yoke" is to be committed to a work which demands all one's strength. In a more pejorative sense, the yoke as used in the gospels is used to express the insupportable burden of the Jewish law as a weight on the people (cf. *Mt.* 23:4). In contrast to this burden of the law, Christ proposes his own "burden" addressed to all men (not just the Jews, as was the case with the law). These men and women are called to be recreated in Christ, to find solace in him since he is *meek* and *humble*. This humility of heart as Christ lived it is part and parcel of the life of the Christian who would follow Christ. The meek will inherit the earth (i.e., the Kingdom) both here below and in eschatological times as well. This "inheriting of the land" is a theme common to the Bible from the call of Abraham, who was promised a new land if he had faith in God (cf. *Gen.* 12:1-2; 15:5; 18:18; 22:17; 28:14; also *Rm.* 4:3; *Gal.* 3:6), up to the time of Christ, when the Jews understood this promise mostly in a political sense (cf. *Acts* 1:6).

* * *

The next beatitude (5:6) concerns those who "hunger and thirst for righteousness."

Blessed are those who hunger and thirst for righteousness, for they shall be satisfied (*Mt.* 5:6).

Once again, we see a certain nuance of difference between Matthew and Luke. Luke (6:21) gives a more material meaning to his words for the reasons we have given above. Matthew, however, makes reference to those who have been emptied by the needs of the heart and soul for the sake of justice. The word "justice" has a particular meaning in Matthew in that it refers to God's rule over the affairs of men on earth, a time of holiness and interior rightness. Thus those who strive to make this rule of God a reality in the affairs of men are included in this beatitude as well as those who wish continually to live a better life in Christ. In Matthew we have a definite eschatological perspective in that the more a man desires to be filled with the goods of the Kingdom, the more he will be satisfied when that Kingdom arrives among men.

The following beatitudes may be termed as "active" ones in that they are directed toward those who *act* in this world and the equality of that action. These latter beatitudes are, however, directed toward the same people as the former ones, but we are now told that they have something positive to do: They must *act* with mercy, make peace, be clean of heart.

* * *

Blessed are the merciful, for they shall obtain mercy (*Mt.* 5:7).

This "mercy" to be shown to others is the same as that which God has for us in loving and reconciling us to himself while we were as yet sinners (cf. *Rm.* 5:6, 8). This is a conscious attitude toward those who are "poor" in the above-mentioned sense. There is a relationship of dependence between God's mercy and forgiveness and our own toward others. Those who are themselves merciful and forgiving will be the object of God's mercy in eschatological times. At the moment of judgment, God will be merciful to those who *do not merit* his mercy but who themselves have been merciful to those who are also undeserving of their mercy, especially of their enemies. This theme of mercy is central to the Christian message and is perhaps one of the hardest Christian injunctions to follow and be obedient to in Christian life. Mercy *must* be shown to those who have done us real wrong, if we are to expect the undeserved mercy of God on the last day. This mutual pardon among Christians is the sure sign of God's mercy and forgiveness upon us now and in eschatological times. There is no question here of "meriting" mercy from God — we are by nature undeserving of it — but an *essential* condition for obtaining this mercy from God is our forgiveness and mercy shown to each other. He who is merciful does not *merit* God's mercy but will — for it is God's promise — obtain that divine mercy. This is a continuous obligation on the part of the Christian, since he is the continuous object of God's mercy.

✼　✼　✼

Blessed are the pure in heart, for they shall see God (*Mt.* 5:8).

The term "pure in heart" is, of course, not to be taken exclusively or even, above all, as those who are sexually chaste. Nor is it simply a matter of exterior purity (the law). In the biblical sense, one who has a pure heart is totally committed, without reserve, to God (cf. *Mt.* 6:22-24; *Ps.* 24:4; 51:4-8). This theme of total commitment to Christ is also to be found in the last part of the Sermon on the Mount where Christ tells us that we cannot belong partly to him and partly to another force (6:24: mammon, money). We must be totally given over to Christ —"Let the dead bury the dead," "you cannot serve two masters," "no one who looks back is fit for the Kingdom," etc.— all expressions which indicate this total commitment. To love with one's whole heart is to "be pure in heart." To give anything less than this is simply not to love Christ, since in such a case he would be a person who merits only part of our attention.

As a reward for this, such a person "will see God," which is a common theme in the Old Testament. This expression means not a sort of "beatific vision," but rather to see the signs of God's actions in history, in the affairs of men. The time of seeing God's truly extraordinary intervention in human history will be on the last day, when he shall act in a definitive manner on behalf of his people. The New Testament specifies this (especially in St. Paul) by saying that on that day we shall see him as he is, that is, we shall have an immediate encounter with him "face to face" (cf. I *Cor*. 13:12).

*　*　*

The second beatitude of action goes as follows:

Blessed are the peacemakers, for they shall be called sons of God (*Mt*. 5:9).

The word "peacemaker" comes directly from the Greek (*erenepoioi*) and designates those men who directly negotiate an end to a war, "those who make peace." This same word is used by St. Paul in *Col*. 1:20 to designate the work of Christ in reconciling man with God. Matthew, however, does not designate here peace ambassadors (even though they are not excluded), but rather those who work to promote peace among men, those who try to bring about union and reconciliation among men.

Peace in the New Testament

The peace which Christ has come to bring to earth (and which, by implication, his followers are to endeavor to bring about) is not simply an interior peace or tranquility "of the soul." This sort of "peace" is

more characteristic of the Stoics and Epicureans than
of Christ. When the Christian looks about him, he
sees all forms of strife, disharmony and oppositions
in the world (war being the end and most brutal result of all of this). He is under divine obligation to
try to reconcile men as much as possible within the
realm of possibility. For Matthew and for the New
Testament, peacemaking is nothing more than a
special application of *fraternal charity*. The Christian
tries to unite people other than himself. Such people
"will be called" children of God since the divine call
for men is to divine sonship of Christ. In *Mt.* 5:45 we
see the requirements of our divine sonship, since, if
we are sons of the common Father, God, we are also
brothers. Here it is not a question of loving only those
whom we like or are related to by blood or kin — but
rather loving those who are indeed difficult to love:
the poor and despised, our enemies and those who
have wronged us. We must go beyond the simple
natural movements of love toward our flesh and blood,
to all men, especially those who are naturally un-
lovable. Thus proof of love here is to attempt to make
peace among brothers; love and peace are signs of
the divine sonship which is ours. Because of this
exercised love in the service of men as brothers, we
shall be proclaimed and be sons of God on the last day.
(To be *called* and *to be* are the same thing in the
Bible.)

In vs. 1-3 Matthew uses the present tense of the
verb while in vs. 4-9 he uses the future. Now, once
again in v. 10 he begins to employ the present, thus
bringing out the dialectic between the present and

the future, between the *now* and the eschatological. In the persecution which Christians endure on behalf of the Kingdom, there is already an experience of happiness which is the sign of the presence of the Kingdom even *now*. Happiness is a sign of the Kingdom in our midst. Thus we read:

> Blessed are you when men revile you and persecute you and utter all kinds of evil against you falsely on my account, rejoice and be glad for your reward is great in heaven (5:11).

We see immediately that his passage must have been composed later than the others, for it bears the marks of a community which has already suffered for the name of Christ. This is evident since, reasonably speaking, there was little persecution of Christ at the beginning of his public life when this sermon was supposed to have been given. The passage was probably written to console those Christians who had already endured sufferings for the name of Christ. To be joined with Christ is to be persecuted and to suffer with him: This is the basic lesson which the Christian must learn. This suffering brings its own joy which the "world" cannot understand, since it lives by different values and objectives than does the Christian (cf. I *Thess.* 3:3-4):

> You yourselves knew that this is to be our lot. For when we were with you, we told you beforehand that we were to suffer affliction; just as it has come to pass, and as you knew.

Indeed, the persecutions which the first Christians faced were in two stages. As is evident from *Acts*, they were first submitted to verbal attacks, false charges of infanticide, sexual aberration, etc. It was only later that bloody persecution became the rule. These persecutions were nothing new even to the Old Testament, where we have the bloody persecutions of the Maccabeans under Antiochus Epiphanus (170-160 B.C.). Jesus applies this same theme to his followers.

A popular Jewish tradition said that all the prophets were martyrs for their faith. Even in the Christian tradition, we have the story that all of the Apostles were prophets. Be that as it may, we do have the very example of Jesus and of the Baptist who were violently put to death. To be a prophet is also to be persecuted; hence those who would follow in his footsteps and cooperate with him in proclaiming the good news of salvation gotten through Christ must know in advance that they will face trials, calumnies and even death itself.

Luke's gospel (6:22-23) has the same beatitude but mentions some of the concrete characteristics of the persecution. Men will hate Christians because of their name, excommunicate them from gatherings — all for the sake of Christ. Yet throughout this persecution runs the theme of joy of imitating Christ. If Christians suffer now for Christ, this is a guarantee of being with Christ at the *parousia*. Christians must be faithful even during those times of persecution as the greatest proof of their love of Christ. Joy in the midst of persecution is a Christian paradox.

Conclusion

These beatitudes are addressed more directly to Christ's disciples than to the crowds. Christ prepares the Apostles for their mission to the world in order to proclaim the good news of salvation. Just as the prophets (who were the messengers of faith to the world) were persecuted because of the Word, so too with the Apostles and the disciples of Christ. This is clear from *Mt.* 10:5-42 which is the sermon of the Mission of the Apostles. We see there the same theme of persecution because of the Word. The follower of Jesus goes to a world with different values from his, under the influence of evil. The struggle between the two is inevitable and may even become tragic.

II
THE OLD AND THE NEW LAW

1. *The Sayings of Good Example*

The beatitudes were an introduction to the whole body of the Sermon on the Mount. We now begin a second section (*Mt.* 5:13-16) which consists of a series of three images by which Christ helps to form the twelve in the sense of their mission. In an indirect way as well, these images are intended for all of the followers of Christ in their Christian witness.

The first image is that of salt (cf. *Mk.* 9:49; *Lk.* 14:34). The text of Mark reads as follows:

For every one will be salted with fire. Salt is good; but if the salt has lost its saltness, how will you season it?

The image of salt was familiar to the people. Its first function was to give savor to food and had a real value when so used. It was also known for its preservative power and, hence, came to be seen as a symbol of fidelity. Thus salt was used to symbolize the eternity of the bond of the Alliance. Salt then has a definite function. If it can no longer fulfill this function, it is useless and must be thrown out. Mark adds the enigmatic: "Have salt in yourselves, and be at peace with one another" (50[b]). This is not understandable and is not kept by either Luke or Matthew.

Luke has the following (14:34-35[a]):

Salt is good; but if salt has lost its taste, how shall its saltness be restored? It is fit neither for the land nor for the dunghill; men throw it away.

We have here the primitive idea that salt will improve the quality of the land and its fertility and thereby promote the growth of crops. Again, salt has a definite function; and if it loses its quality, it is good for nothing.

Matthew has the following (5:13):

You are the salt of the earth; but if salt has lost its taste, how shall its saltness be restored? It is no longer good for anything except to be thrown out and trodden under foot.

The perspective here is wider than in Mark or Luke. The Mission of the Apostles is to the whole world, and they must keep the evangelical message alive and fertile. This mission makes certain demands on the Apostles which, if they do not fulfill them, render them worthless. Christ does not say that this unfruitful

Apostle will be condemned, but only that he is useless for the apostolate (cf. I *Cor.* 3:15).

The Apostles are told that by the good news which they give to the world, they will be giving that world its meaning and its sense. If they do not bring their own efforts and example to this work, they will be worthless and a scandal to that world.

The second image which Christ uses is that of a city and of light (*Mt.* 5:14-15):

> You are the light of the world. A city set on a hill cannot be hid. Nor do men light a lamp and put it under a bushel but on a stand and it gives light to all in the house.

Only Matthew uses the image of the city which was very common in the Mediterranean area. A city so situated was visible to all who came near.

The image of the lamp is also familiar to the ancients (cf. *Mk.* 4:21). A bushel was a measuring pot for grain or liquid. It was a "must" for every household — even the poorest. All of these examples are found in the homes of all — a lamp, an earthen jar, a bed, a lampstand. Thus Christ addresses himself even to the very poor.

The gospel of Luke gives us the image of the lamp in a slightly different form in 8:16; to the words of Matthew, he adds the words: "That those who enter may see the light"— which is clarified in 11:33: "No one after lighting a lamp puts it in a cellar or under a bushel, but on a stand, that those who enter may see the light." That is, a missionary activity is given here so that others may participate in the light. The "house" here is the community of the Church enlightened by the good example of Christians.

The account cited above of *Mt.* 5:15-16 does not mention the bed and ends in the same way as that of Luke: "so that it may shine for all those (who are) in the house." It is evident that, contrary to Luke, the emphasis is upon those who are already *in the house.* Only Matthew has the conclusion (v.16): "Let your light so shine before men, that they may see your good works and give glory to your Father who is in heaven." The general idea is that we must help one another in fraternal charity and example in the house first (Church) and then to go out to others. Whereas Luke speaks of those (pagans) who come into the house and see the good works of Christians, Matthew says that those in the house must perform good works, in order to be an example to each other first with the result that, from there, they can go out to all men who will then praise the Father who is in heaven. Witness to the world (in both accounts) is a vital point of the Christian message.

2. *The Saying of Antitheses*

In this section, we have a whole series of comparisons between the Old and the New Law so that Christ's words are seen not as a destruction of the Old (which is pre-supposed) but as its fulfillment and perfection. We see this throughout the section (*Mt.* 5:17-48). The section is interspersed with some related examples of what Christ is talking about (5:23-26, 29-30, 45-48).

We are first given the basic principles to follow in all of these cases (vs. 17-20): the Old Law is imperfect but is not, for all that, to be destroyed. It is to be perfected by the New Law (fraternal charity) given by Christ:

> Think not that I have come to abolish the law and the prophets; I have come not to abolish them but "to fulfill" (*plerosai*) them.

The words "to fulfill" or "to bring to completion" has a very particular meaning in Matthew. This same phrase is given to us at the baptism of Jesus by the Baptist (3:15):

> Let it be so now; for thus it is fitting to fulfill all righteousness (*plerosai pasan dikaiosunen*).

The word *"pleron"* (to fulfill) is a word used very often by Matthew and less by Mark and Luke (16, 2, 9 times respectively). Each time that it is used in the gospel, it refers to a fulfillment of an Old Testament text or prophecy. The sense of continuation is implied in the text so that the fulfillment contains the Old but also its completion in the New. The original intent of the Old is brought boldly into view and is given its ultimate completion in the New.

The word "justice" or "righteousness" which appears in the Sermon on the Mount has a very special meaning for Matthew. The Old Testament idea of justice signified man's conformity to the will of God as expressed in and through his law. We today, perhaps, would use the term "holiness" to express what the ancients meant by the term "justice" (*dikoimenon*). The reason the Old Testament would not have used a word such as "holiness" to express this relationship is that holiness was not a virtue but a special gift of God that permitted one to share in the very life of God.

Both of these terms together express a unique idea in *Mt.* 3:15 (as well as its use in the Sermon on the Mount). In submitting to the baptism of John, Jesus not only performed an act of justice, but he also brought to completion and perfection the whole Old Testament of which its rite of baptism was only a symbol of purification. Christ gives that symbol its ultimate and spiritual meaning. In Christ, the rite of baptism with water becomes that reality by which the Holy Spirit effectively comes to man. This new Baptism now actually bestows (not just symbolizes) the sanctifying gift of the Spirit to the followers of Jesus. Their behavior — following from this living and dynamic relationship with God — must also be just and holy. The morality of Christians flows from the fact that they are as sons of God. The just man who does the will of God has made him just. This justice of Christians, says Christ, must exceed the justice of the Scribes and Pharisees — whose teachings were not abolished by Christ. This would be no easy task since their teachings were rigorous and demanding.

In the following two verses, we run across a major difficulty in Matthew where he seems to be contradicting himself. The question which is implicitly posited here was: Can we forget about the precepts of the Old Law? This was a vexing problem for the primitive Christian community and was to disturb the whole period of New Testament composition (47-66 A.D.). Matthew gives an ambiguous answer:

For truly I say to you, till heaven and earth pass away, not an iota, not a dot, will pass from the law until all is accomplished (5:18).

The answer here is quite clear and affirmative: no precept of the law can be done away with until its perfection in the New — not even in its most minute details. This is a strictly orthodox rabbinical interpretation of the law. Yet:

Whoever then relaxes one of the least of these commandments and teaches men so, shall be called least in the Kingdom of heaven; but he who does them and teaches them shall be called great in the Kingdom of heaven (5:19).

Here we find a subtle distinction: the man who violates the "little laws" will be called least in the Kingdom of heaven. He will enter the Kingdom but will occupy a secondary place within it. The man who obeys and teaches even these little laws will have a preeminent place in the Kingdom.

Here we see the whole conflict between Palestinian Jews converted to Christianity and the pagans who were also converted. There was a basic tension between these two groups (cf. *Acts* 15:6-29; *Gal.* 2:1-10).

The basic meaning of the entire passage is in vs. 17 and 20 where the general principle is enunciated: we must fulfill the law by going beyond it in the New. In vs. 18-19 we have reflected the historical situation of the Christian community which, for a time, led a sort of double life. The community of Jerusalem kept the law, went to the temple to pray (cf. *Acts* 3:1) and met together for the celebration of the Christian liturgy. This "Jewish party" insisted that Christ did not abolish the Old Law (which therefore had to be observed) but only perfected it. There was another group of Christians converted from Judaism mostly from the diaspora (of whom Stephen was a major figure, *Acts* 7:2-60), who pointed out that many prescriptions of the law were truly small and secondary matters — of little consequence to the Christian. These could be set aside according to the words of Jesus, v.g., the words of Christ concerning the Sabbath.

In view of all this there was at least some confusion especially to those who would eventually be converted to the Church. The present verses (18-19) are an attempt at a synthesis or reconciliation between these two groups. In other words, what these verses are saying is that the most perfect Christians keep the law in its totality (every little prescription), while others disregard them but do all that is necessary for salvation. It is no wonder that Mark and Luke preserve nothing of this whole discussion for us.

Thus the law, or torah (Pentateuch), which was the expression of God's will for men was emphasized by the rabbis who tended to forget or play down the influence of the prophetical tradition of Israel. For all practical purposes, the rabbis at the time of Christ tended to neglect the prophets by over-emphasizing the role of the law. The law alone was sufficient for salvation and indeed contained the totality of God's will for man.

Christ, on the other hand, while not neglecting the role of the law, stressed the prophetical tradition as well. As a matter of fact, he claims to accomplish their work, since the law is not complete in itself. It needs the prophets whose living continuation Christ is. Without this fulfillment, the law can only crush and destroy people by the sheer weight of its many obligations. Thus the law *by itself* cannot accomplish one's justice. The Israelite must go beyond the law to its fulfillment which only Christ brings. This can only be accomplished by going beyond the law to God and to Christ, who alone can give the strength for obedience to the law in its perfection. Christ points out (*Mt.* 5:17) that the law is imperfect and that he comes to perfect the law. Christ now gives the perfect revelation which will accomplish the law's justice. The New Law of Christ is not simply better than the Old; it will be perfect in its own right. Christ goes beyond the law in order to bring it to its fulfillment. This presupposes something new as given by Jesus. All is not in the law; and Christ is not simply another or a *new* prophet; Christ is actually here giving a whole new mentality, a whole new way of life which surpasses that of the Old Testament but presupposes it as a foundation stone from which to build. Jesus declares the very will of God directly to the people (not a commentary, new or otherwise, of the law as did the Scribes and Pharisees). Christ possesses a perfect knowledge of the will of God since he is capable of seeing the law as God sees it, in the whole of God's plan. He dared to question the imperfection of the law and to give it a fuller and more perfect meaning. He gives us an entirely new attitude toward the law. This action of Christ is more than any prophet of the Old Testament ever dared to do; it points to the unique personality of Jesus and of his very special relationship to God. This whole discourse on the law and its fulfillment forces us to ask the question of Jesus: "Who is he?" How could he have known the will of God so perfectly? Already, then, this sermon leaves us wondering about the person of Christ.

What are these differences between the Old and the New Law? The following section (vs. 21-48) attempts to give us an answer to this question. The Old Testament quotations used here are classical in that they refer to the decalogue as found in *Exodus,* Chapter 21 and *Deuteronomy,* Chapter 5.

The first antithesis (vs. 21-22):

You have heard it said to the men of Old, "You shall not kill; and whoever kills shall be liable to judgment." But I say to you that everyone who is angry with his brother shall be liable to judgment; whoever insults his brother shall be liable to the council, and whoever says, "You fool" shall be liable to the hell of fire.

The basic format to be followed throughout these passages is clear here: Christ cites the law and pushes it further in the same direction. Thus: the law commanded not to kill. The meaning of the Hebrew is "to murder," for it did not concern the killing of adversaries in the "holy war" (even women and children) and did not affect legitimate self defense pre-supposed in the law. What was forbidden in the law was the private execution of justice against one's enemies. But Christ goes further than this commandment. Even he who is angry with his brother (v. 22ª) will be condemned to the same fate as a murderer. It is not anger itself which is here being condemned; rather it is anger directed toward a brother as a serious breach of fraternal charity. Furthermore, the word "raka" is not just a sign of anger but anger expressed in an insulting and abusive way to the brother. The word has here (22ᵇ) the connotation of scorn. A person who scorns his brother shall be subject to the Sanhedrin, or the ruling body of the Jews. Moreover, whoever says "You fool" to his brother is at once insulting and abusing the brother. It is tantamount to saying that he is a good-for-nothing or absolutely useless person. Such a person will be "liable to the hell of fire" (literally, *Gehenna*). The word *Gehenna* comes from a valley south of Jerusalem where once was located the altar to the god of Moloch to whom were sacrificed live children. Thus the word came to designate a place of punishment for sinners who persisted in their evil.

We may say that in going beyond the letter of the law, Christ has gone to the very source of those things forbidden by the law: the interior man, the heart and soul of a man. This spoken word of anger, of scorn — at least among the Orientals of that time — was considered to be effective in bringing about what it signified. That is why the penalties which Christ gives out for these seemingly slight offenses (which seem so insignificant to us) were very serious for the men and women of Christ's time (cf. *James* 3:1-12, where the effects of the tongue are so forcefully brought out). He who controls his tongue is indeed a perfect man since, in Hebrew thought, the spoken word is the very symbol and vehicle of the thought of the heart. For the Hebrew, to think and to speak are almost the same thing. The root of all violence, of all hatred which destroys fraternal charity, resides in the heart of man which expresses itself in words. Such thoughts lead to murder, adultery, etc. Our Lord gives us the practical conclusion of this offense against fraternal charity:

> So if you are offering your gift at the altar, and there remember that your brother has something against you, leave your gift there before the altar and go; first be reconciled with your brother, and then come and offer your gift (vs. 23-24).

Matthew has artificially placed these verses here. They do not belong here either chronologically or logically. This is seen if we note that, whereas Christ in the preceding verses, uses the third person plural ("all who"), he now uses the second person singular — hardly a way of addressing a large crowd. But there is a certain connection even if this phrase is artificially set up by the evangelist. The reason for the injunction of the law is fraternal charity, and without this the

New Law is destroyed and eviscerated. This same theme is given in *Mk.* 11:25:

> And whenever you stand praying, forgive, if you have anything against anyone; so that your Father also who is in Heaven may forgive you your trespasses.

Mark does not mention the offering at the temple as does Matthew but stresses personal prayer. The *Our Father* is referred to in this passage but has been changed somewhat to read "your" instead of "our." The idea is that the sincerity of any prayer before God will be measured by the extent or degree that there is forgiveness and reconciliation with our brothers. *Fraternal charity is the essential criteria of our sincerity before God, our Father.* The context of Mark is more logical than that of Matthew. In a sense, this tradition of sacrifice without sincerity and conversion of heart was common in Israel particularly in the prophetical tradition (cf. *Isaiah* 1:11-19; *Amos* 8:9-10). All formalistic sacrifices are rejected as abominations before the sight of God. The sacrifices of a man or a people who oppressed the poor and needy were a stench before God and were accordingly rejected. The only sacrifice acceptable to God must begin with the heart and mind and is born of fraternal charity and love of God. There can be no liturgy without fraternal charity. Matthew repeats that any liturgy must of necessity begin with a reconciliation of brothers before we dare to approach God, our Father.

Then there follows a sort of prudential mode of action (vs. 25-26):

Make friends quickly with your accuser, while you are going with him to court, lest your accuser hand you over to the judge, and the judge to the guard, and you be put in prison; truly I say to you, you will never get out till you have paid the last penny.

It is more like an adage from *Wisdom* literature giving general advice: if you have a dispute with an adversary, try to settle out of court on your way to the judge, because if you don't, you might go through the whole legal process and get condemned. This is one interpretation.

There is another interpretation possible which is eschatological in nature. Just as in this life, we shall be condemned if we do not reconcile ourselves with our brothers, so too our failure to be reconciled with him in this life by fraternal charity will result in our condemnation on the last day.

Luke has a parallel passage in 12:58-59 which is almost the same as that of Matthew. Yet, it is within a whole context of eschatological interpretation of our present passage.

12:16 gives us the story of the rich man who had so many goods that he had to build more barns to hold them all. Not using his goods for fraternal charity, he is called to God that very night and is thus unprepared to meet God.

12:32-40 — Christ gives admonitions to his listeners to become attentive to his words now so that they will not be condemned on the last day.

12:49-56 — these scenes are apocalyptic in terms as to prepare for the last day.

It is therefore natural to intepret vs. 58-59 of *Lk.* 12 in an eschatological perspective, and since it is the same saying as in Matthew, it is natural to presuppose that at least a possible interpretation of Matthew is also an eschatological one.

The second antithesis is found in *Mt.* 5:27-30:

> You have heard that it was said "You shall not commit adultery?" But I say to you that every one who looks at a woman lustfully has already committed adultery with her in his heart. If your right eye causes you to sin, pluck it out and throw it away; it is better that you lose one of your members than that your whole body be thrown into hell.

The sixth commandment of the decalogue is clearly given which forbids sexual relations with one who is not one's wife. In the Old Testament adultery was considered an injustice against the husband since he was the exclusive owner of his wife. She was his property, and a "woman" here is understood as a married woman. Just as with the spoken word which we mentioned above, so too with a look. A look was seen by the ancients as an act which directs one's whole personality to God or to a certain goal. Thus a lustful look at a woman is identified as an act, since it comes from the heart and mind — it is a start toward adultery, for adultery first begins in the heart (that is why oriental women, even to this day, wear a veil over their faces — to prevent such "looks").

The "eye" and the "hand" which are to be removed lest they lead us to sin is metaphorical to indicate the extreme measures we must take to guard ourselves against evil. The "eye" sees from the heart and the hand executes what the eye has begun. The right hand is mentioned for the simple reason that most men use their right hand for action. Certain actions can be the cause of the destruction of our whole moral person. Therefore, if we do not act with vigor against such tendencies, our whole person will be condemned on the last day. An interior, as well as an exterior chastity, is demanded by Christ, since chastity is first of all and foremost a matter of the heart and not of the body.

The next verses in Matthew have caused some of the greatest difficulties of interpretation concerning marriage and divorce:

> It was also said, "Whoever divorces his wife, let him give her a certificate of divorce." But I say to you that everyone who divorces his wife, except on the grounds of unchastity (fornication), makes her an adultress; and whoever marries a divorced woman commits adultery (vs. 31-32).

The composition and style of this passage is much like those which have immediately preceded. There is, however, one major difference: while the above antitheses refer directly to the commandments of the decalogue, there can be found no commandment like the one which Christ mentions here. Many commentators claim that these two verses do not belong to the Sermon on the Mount. Be that as it may, there are parallel passages in the other gospels (cf. *Mk.* 10:11-12 and *Lk.* 16:18).

We must first investigate some background to this whole question. The Old Testament in fact did permit divorce in certain circumstances: indecency or lewdness in the wife was sufficient for this purpose (cf. *Deut.* 24:1). These reasons were eventually extended to include almost any dislike of the wife. The reasoning behind *Deuteronomy* permitting divorce must be seen in the context of ancient oriental culture. The wife's role was to bear and educate children to insure the continuation of the husband and the tribe. It was only in this way that economic patrimony could be secured in primitive societies. If she became pregnant by another man, the legitimacy of his children came into doubt with its corresponding effects on the economy and reputation of the husband. This could not be tolerated and the usual penalty was death, later substituting divorce for death ("a bill of divorce"). This allowed her to return to her parents and to marry again, if she found someone else. A worse penalty was to send her home without her freedom. At the time of Christ, there were two interpretations concerning the possibility of divorce:

1. The one was a strict interpretation of the biblical text (*Deut.* 24:1). A woman may be divorced only in case of adultery. In such cases, the man could release her to go back to her parents free to marry, if she could find another man.

2. The second was a more or less laxist view of the

matter, permitting divorce for almost anything at all, v.g., if she were no longer pleasing to her husband.

It is within such a context that the question is put to Christ, that is, whether he was a rigorist or a laxist. Christ, however, chooses neither of these two positions and goes beyond them: he forbids all divorce.

This same theme of divorce and remarriage can be seen in *Mt.* 19:9, *Mk.* 10:11-12 and *Lk.* 16:18. Both of these latter evangelists report the same words as Matthew except that they eliminate the words: "except in case of adultery (fornication)." It would be worth our time to examine what each of the other evangelists has to say in this regard:

Mk. 10:1-12:

And the Pharisees in order to test him asked, "Is it lawful for a man to divorce his wife?" He answered them, "What did Moses command you?" They said, "Moses allowed a man to write a certificate of divorce, and to put her away." But Jesus said to them, "From your hardness of heart he wrote you this commandment. But from the beginning of creation, 'God made them male and female.' 'For this reason a man shall leave his father and mother and be joined to his wife, and the two shall become one.' So they are no longer two but one. What therefore God has joined together, let not man put asunder."

And in the house the disciples asked him again about this matter. And he said to them, "Whoever divorces his wife and marries another, commits adultery against her; and if she divorces her husband and marries another, she commits adultery."

The gospel of Mark situates the words of Christ within two contexts. In the first part of the passage (vs. 2-9) Christ is in a controversy with the Pharisees (much as we saw above between the rigorists and the laxists). The second section is given in private to his disciples (vs. 10-12).

Jesus gives no direct answer to the question of the Pharisees. The answer of the Pharisees was a reference to *Deut.* 24, which permitted divorce. Jesus goes back still further to the original intention of God in instituting marriage in *Gen.* 1:27 and 2:24. Originally God made man and woman fundamentally equal. She was not solely for children (even if she were to give him children as is evident from *Gen.* 1:27), but she was also to be a companion to man and his complement (cf. *Gen.* 2:24). Before woman's creation, man was alone and she was created to be his companion. She is, therefore, an equal, and not a slave or servant like the other animals. She breaks into his loneliness and for this reason Adam jumps for joy. Even the Hebrew word for woman (*isha*) is taken from the word "man" (*ish*). She was taken from the same "flesh" as Adam, therefore implying an equality of nature.

We have in these biblical quotes given by Christ the themes of equality, companionship and love in married life. For this, a man will leave mother and father and "cleave to his wife" because they are inseparable and the marriage is indissoluble. They form one moral person joined together by God. No man has the power (human power) to dissolve a marriage. Divorce is therefore forbidden and in order to arrive at this intention of the Scriptures, Christ authentically interprets the meaning of these texts by going directly to the intention of the author — God.

To sum up, the Old Testament teaching on marriage as found in *Genesis* was not put into practice in Israel. Polygamy was allowed and divorce was permitted "because of the hardness of their hearts." This flowed from the fact that women were considered only means of reproduction, thereby misinterpreting the very message of *Genesis*. From time to time, the ideal was appealed to in the prophetic tradition (*Malachi* 2:14), but this was considered to be simply an ideal, not an obligatory directive for the people. Jesus, however goes back to the original teaching of *Genesis* and the indissolubility of the marriage covenant. In order to do this, he gives us the authentic teaching which God meant in that passage. For his followers, there can be no divorce where both partners are equal (cf. *Lk.* 16:18).

There remains one disturbing addition (which is authentic and contained in the best manuscripts) which appears both in *Mt.* 5:32 and 19:9: "except for immorality" (*parektos logou porneias*). The Greek word "porneia" meant originally a prostitute or prostitution but was used by the Christian community for any sexual misconduct. Apparently, Matthew is giving us an evident exception to the absolute law of Christ forbidding divorce. In case of sexual misconduct on the part of the wife, the man is permitted to divorce her. Is then, remarriage permitted in such a circumstance?

Could this be an interjection of Matthew reflecting the primitive Christian community (Jewish) on this crucial matter? Many Scholars see here a hesitance of the first Christians — mostly Jewish — to pass from the Old to the New Testament, since both Mark and Luke have almost the same words but *without* this addition. The argument of these scholars would be as follows: these Christians felt obligated to follow the words and actions of Christ, but they were not certain whether and to what extent they should leave the Jewish law aside. Jesus surpassed the content of the Old Law in many ways, and the spirit of his teaching certainly seems to rule out all divorce. These Christians, however, felt that he would not have abrogated this aspect of the Old Law and added this exception.

Christian tradition — even during the time of the composition of the New Testament itself — rules out all divorce and remarriage, since *none* of the other writers of the New Testament conserve this exception for us.[1] It is indeed a *hapax* (done only once) of the New Testament and must be explained, as we have indicated, within the historical context of the primitive Christian community of Jewish origins and its relationship to the Jewish law.

1. There is an exception. Greek Orthodox churches at least from the third century permitted divorce and remarriage in case of adultery on the part of either couple. They argue from the text of Matthew, and this custom continues even today among the Greek Orthodox churches. Catholic explanations of this text, trying to explain this exception of Matthew, have been precarious (scripturally) to say the least.

The third antithesis of Matthew goes as follows (vs. 33-37):

Again you have heard that it was said to the men of old, "You shall not swear falsely, but shall perform to the Lord what you have sworn." But I say to you, do not swear at all, either by heaven for it is the throne of God, or by the earth for it is his footstool, or by Jerusalem, for it is the city of the great king. And do not swear by your head, for you cannot make one hair white or black. Let what you say be simply "Yes" or "No"; anything more than this comes from evil.

There are two sections present here —vs. 33-34 and vs. 35-37. Let us take them in logical order.

Vs. 33-34: We have here a simple restatement of the law with a going beyond the law by words of Christ. A false oath was considered to be a mockery of God, since the one who takes such an oath calls upon God to be a witness that what he is saying is the truth. Examples of this can be found in the Old Testament such as *Gen.* 15:17-21 and *Jeremiah* 34:8-9. In these cases, for instance, the two halves of a cut animal symbolized what should happen to the one or the other party, if he did not keep his word. (With the case of God, the covenant is always unilateral to show his mercy, favor and gratuity in choosing.)

The answer of Jesus is in a threefold reply to buttress his central contention that his followers should not swear at all. He gives the ordinary referential points of Jewish oaths and argues against each of them:

—"not by heaven" since it is God's throne; it belongs exclusively to God, and we therefore have no right to exercise any authority over it — even in the form of an oath.

—"not by the earth for it is God's footstool." In this oriental vision, God has complete dominion over the earth as depicted in the images of a conquering king who puts his enemies under his feet. We have various representations in archeology of the Egyptian Pharaohs putting their feet upon their conquered enemies (cf. *Ps.* 110:1).

—"nor by Jerusalem for it is the city of the great king." This can be understood as referring to David but more probably to God himself, since only God was the true king of the Israelites.

—"nor by your own head." We cannot swear over something that simply is not ours; even our destinies and our own bodies belong exclusively to God.

Thus a person may not swear because he has no power over God to use him for his own ends, since God is not the servant of man. We tend to invoke the name of God superficially, not recognizing the gravity of what we are doing, and thus lose the awareness of God's dignity and transcendence. Therefore, we ought to avoid taking God's name loosely or superficially.

With regard to oaths taken on other things (e.g., Jerusalem, our head, heaven and earth), the same principle applies here as well: none of these things belongs to us, nor are they at our unrestricted disposal. Here we see the fundamental *poverty* of man who depends on God every moment of his being for *everything* he has and is. Since none of these things is his own, he cannot swear by them.

V. 37 concludes this whole antithesis with Christ stating that the words we use must be used in honesty to convey the truth, not duplicity or lies. They should manifest what is in our hearts or they are falsities and damnable, since in Hebrew thought the word and the heart are (or should be) very closely associated. Christ says that anything else is "from evil," and since this word is used in the Greek dative case, it can be understood as referring either to the devil or to the neuter, evil. If a man is true to himself, his words will be true and sincere. This will be sufficient proof of a man's sincerity and honesty, and he will not need an external authority to vouch for the truth he speaks. We need no other authority than our truthful word.

The fourth antithesis concerns the law of Talion (*Mt.* 5:38-42):

> You heard that it was said, "An eye for an eye and a tooth for a tooth." But I say to you, do not resist one who is evil. But if anyone strike you on the right cheek, turn to him the other also; and if anyone should sue you and take your coat, let him have your cloak as well; and if anyone forces you to go one mile, go with him two miles. Give to him who begs from you, and do not refuse him who would borrow from you.

Christ first gives us the Old Law of Talion given in *Lev.* 19-20. It might seem surprising, but this law was set down in an attempt to humanize violence among men. If a man breaks my arm, I may *only* break his arm; the natural tendency in most men is to give back more than they get, even to kill a man for the breaking of an arm (cf. the Vendetta of Lamech in *Gen.* 4:23). This was progress in society since ancient times were simply ruled on the premise of superior force. It would at least prevent wholesale slaughter of innocent people in ancient rituals of punishment such as the vendetta, common among Semitics in particular. The thinking underlying this mentality was that if a person did not respond in kind, the whole family or clan would be in danger of attack and destruction with no fear of reprisal. We have here the "balance of terror" keeping a certain equilibrium among an uncivilized and unlawful people. It is this sense of self protection which was codified in what is known as the "law of Talion."

Christ's directives to his followers are truly revolutionary by going beyond this law. We should not resist an evil person when he attacks us, and then he gives us the details (the other cheek, gift of the tunic as well, etc.). This must have created a shock (as indeed it still does if one preaches this today), for the normal thing to do when attacked is to defend oneself against the attacker. To give up one's cloak was a great thing indeed, for among the poor this was the great garment used for almost everything, inclusive of keeping warm at night when it became very cold (e.g., *Deut.* 24:10-13, the law permitted a man to take another man's cloak for collateral but had to return it before nightfall so the man could sleep in it for warmth). The forcing of "a mile" was an ancient custom of the civil authority who could requisition labor on the spot for some needy work (e.g., soldiers, repairmen). This is seen in *Mt.* 27:32 where the authorities forced Simon the Cyrene to help Jesus carry his cross.

V. 42 refers to the natural greed and possessiveness of men with regard to their goods and rights. Men tend to emphasize what is theirs to an extreme degree even if it means less or nothing for others. The law of Jesus is different from this form of natural possessiveness. We must view the other as a person (not a thing to be used for our own advantage) who has needs as we do. In laying claim to my rights, I often overlook the other and thereby cease to live in the community of true brotherhood. From this comes struggle and contention in the community. The followers of Jesus must be continuously vigilant for the needs of others, even to the degree of self sacrifice on their part.

Thus we see here the very foundation of the New Law is one of *non-violence,* which is still, as yet, to be put into practice by Christians today. This does not abrogate the ancient law of legitimate self-defense, but it does introduce a new spirit of peace and harmony, and Christians, above all others, must be the sign of this reconciling non-violence in history. The essential meaning of the words of Christ is that Christians must be constantly vigilant as to the needs of others as a mark and manifestation of fraternal charity even to giving up the insistence on our own rights. This may seem strong to us, but then Christ here goes beyond simply natural ethics to the basic Christian ethic of love. This is summed up for us in the next antithesis of Matthew (vs. 43-48):

> You have heard that it was said, "You shall love your neighbor and hate your enemy." But I say to you, love your enemies and pray for those who persecute you, so that you may be sons of your Father who is in heaven; for he makes his sun rise on the evil and on the good, and sends rain on the just and the unjust. For if you love those who love you, what reward have you? Do not even the tax collectors do the same? And if you salute only your brethren, what more are you doing than others? Do not even the Gentiles do the same? You therefore must be perfect, as your heavenly Father is perfect.

The Old Law which Christ states is taken from *Lev.* 19:18 in which all morality is related to God's sanctity, since the first verse of this chapter starts with the phrase: "Be you holy, because I, the Lord, your God am holy." The "neighbor" as used in this text is a brother, or at least a fellow citizen (a compatriot). V. 18 of *Leviticus* forbids vengeance or the holding of grudges against the children of their own people, followed by the command to love the neighbor (18b) or the people near us. In context, it refers to the people of Israel. The reason for this is simple: We are to love them as we love ourselves because *they are* ourselves, since we form one people with them. Love is essentially related to another, and in this case it is one's friends, relatives, fellow citizens, all of whom form the same people. People outside of the tribe or clan cannot be loved since they are foreigners, strangers to our ways and customs. (They are even the enemy, since even the Latin word for stranger [*hostis*] also means an enemy.) These we must "hate," which means in Hebrew thought, to love less. It does not mean the act of positively acting against another as we normally use the word in English. Thus in *Gen.* 29:21-23, it says that Jacob "despised Leah," and from the context it is evident that he loves her less than Rachel. In *Deut.* 21:15 it is a question of two wives of a man, one of which he "hates," which means in context to love one less than the other. This same expression is used in the New Testament in *Lk.* 14:26: "If anyone comes to me and does not hate his own father and mother and wife and children and brothers and sisters, yes, and even his own life, he cannot be my disciple" (cf. also *Mt.* 10:37). It is evident that the Greek word (*missein*) means to love these people less than we do Jesus. The fact of the matter is that nowhere in the Scriptures do we find any command to "hate" anyone in the Western sense of the word.

We find this same phenomenon in some of the texts which have been found in the Caves of Qumran (Dead Sea Scrolls). The rule of the community there as given to us in the literary work, *The Book of Disciples,* says: "You shall love good and hate evil"; "love those who are good and hate those who are evil" (I *QS.* 1, 4). In the first sentence it means "hate" in the strong sense of the word and in the second sentence, the biblical "to love less."

Christ's words go beyond this rather narrow concept of love to a universal and all-inclusive form of love for *all* men, irrespective of who they are. He says, first of all, that we must *pray* for them, especially those who are our enemies, to love is to do good to a person and the greatest good we could possibly wish for another is his salvation in spite of what he has done to us personally. This is perhaps the purest form of love we can show to another. Prayer for a believing Jew was not a form of magical ritual or incantation like the pagans, but was the purest form of doing good to and for another. Prayer required total commitment and dedication to God. In this conception it is impossible to hate and pray. They are contradictory terms. A Jew could do a good turn for another without loving him, but this was impossible for prayer. One could even do good to a person while yet despising him (*Proverbs* 25:21) so that he will be condemned on judgment day. True prayer involves action for good but not vice-versa.

The reason we must love is so that we may become like God, our Father (v. 45). The Greek used here is perhaps even more clear than the English: ". . . so that you may *become* (*genesthe*) sons of your Father." The reasoning is as follows: (1) God is your Father in heaven (he is transcendent). (2) You are on earth (here below, limited). (3) You become his children (by loving, doing good, praying, etc.).

Thus God's children are those who imitate him (v. 48). God is our Father and we are his sons *only to the extent* that we live as he does, and God loves all men irrespective of who they are and what their condition is. This is illustrated by the example which Christ gives of God who makes his sun to shine on the good and on the evil and his rain to fall on the just and the unjust.

Evil in the Old Testament

In the earliest texts of the Bible we find that which is found in almost all religions: God rewards good and he punishes evil while men are as yet on earth. This was known as divine retribution and was a great factor in much of Jewish and Hebrew thought (cf. Book of *Job*). Yet there was the evident problem of the fact that the evil men oftentimes prospered and the good often had a bad lot in life. Hebrew thought often grappled with this thought in the biblical texts. To explain this, various answers were given:

— One response held that the evil man would pay a great price on the last day. If God punished the evil immediately, many innocent people would be unjustly touched by this retribution. God then permits the evil to remain with the good until the last day (this was the whole argument of Abraham in *Gen.* 18:23-33: "For the sake of ten I will not destroy the city").

— Another theory said that God withheld immediate retribution for the wicked in order to give them time to repent while they yet lived. This same theme was taken up by the New Testament as well (cf. *Rm.* 2:4; II *Peter* 3:9). If they persist in their evil, divine retribution will be theirs on the last day.

— A third explanation was that God lets men sin

evermore on earth so that they will have a worse punishment on the last day.

— A variation of the second theory is that God permits evil men to live in order that his love may bring about the conversion of sinners.

None of these speculations is present in the present text of Matthew. There is no eschatology present here with regard to evil or, indeed, for the just. Christ's view is that God is love, and he gives it to all men, both those who deserve it (just) and those who do not (unjust). The mission of his followers must be to become evermore like their Father in this same love. God, who is transcendent, is manifested now to men by his love; Christians become like him who is the "totally other" by imitating this love of his. This was a different emphasis from that of the rabbis of the time who taught that man's fundamental religious obligation was to know and be submissive to the law. Christ did not destroy the law but made its spirit and heart an ethic of love of God and men. The Jewish mind of the time did not emphasize this "imitation" of God, who was transcendent (even if *Gen.* 1:26 said that man is made in God's image and likeness). Even in this text of *Genesis,* man's likeness to God was in dominating the earth, not in a moral sense as we have in *Mt.* 5:45. Thus the revelation of Jesus here is truly revolutionary.

Christ then goes on to give a few examples of the kind of self-centered love which even sinners and pagans have (vs. 46-47). Christ does not call this form of love bad but that he wants his followers to go beyond this, if they are to be imitators and sons of the Father. If Christians only love those who love them in return, they are no better than the normal natural man, since Christ calls them to a higher vocation, to have a universal love like that of God, the Father. Christ uses the term "tax collector" as an expression which told of sin in a most excellent way. They beat and cheated people at will and the Jews considered them sinners *par excellence*. Yet even this group of men had a certain solidarity among themselves since they loved those who loved them. If sinners could do this, how much more must Christians do? Even the pagans have an egotistical form of love, since they help those who help them. If the Christians remain only at this level (love of family, relatives, people, nation, etc.), they cannot measure up to the standards demanded of those who would be sons of God. This indeed is a "hard saying," but this is the demand made by Jesus himself on those who would be his followers. Thus, the conclusion of Matthew: "Be perfect even as your heavenly Father is perfect" (v. 48). This verse is similar to *Lk.* 6:36 which says: "Be merciful, even as your Father is merciful." This formula of Luke is probably the oldest, since it is the mercy of God which we must imitate. It was this mercy — out of love, to be sure — which was shown to men in Christ "while we were as yet sinners" (*Rm.* 5:8). Mercy in the Bible is a capacity of pardon and love of our enemies and is possible only by and through the grace of God. We are all the object of God's absolute and gratuitous mercy, and it is in function of this virtue and by practicing this virtue that we become like God, sons of God.

Matthew substituted the word "perfect" for "merciful" for a number of reasons (even if its message is fundamentally the same as that of Luke). The Greek word "perfect" (*teleos*) means that which is firm and sure or what is mature. It also meant, in Hebrew thought, that which is innocent and pure, without flaw (as the sacrificial victim); but most of all, it meant the plenitude of a quality — in this case, that of love. It is this meaning, in v. 48, which has love being the expression and accomplishment of everything that has been said in the whole Sermon on the Mount. The ethic and vitalizing principle of everything Christ has said is that of love.

Summary

We may summarize what has been said so far in the following way.

The Sermon is a collection of sayings of Jesus arranged together here in one place by Matthew. They are artificially placed here to give us a total whole, a sort of primitive Christian catechism which presents the essential sayings of Jesus, even if it does not give us the totality of his preaching. Christ gives a whole new style and spirit of life animated at its center by love in imitating God. The teaching is not systematic, but a living for Christ who came to give us not a systematic theology but a new way of life.

It is evident throughout this chapter that Jesus knows the will of God perfectly as he goes beyond the law, sometimes giving us the original meaning of the law. Indeed, in some cases there is a certain opposition

(vs. 17-20) between the two ways of life of the New and the Old Law; yet in most cases it is a question of fulfillment, not of opposition. Jesus was able to do this because he knew God's will better than anyone in the Old Testament. His revelation is a revelation of the perfect will of God for men. He does this not by the "law" understood in the Jewish sense, but by a fundamentally different spirit which is that of imitation of God in and through love.

The beatitudes are, therefore, a mission for the followers of Jesus, and the Kingdom makes these *demands* on the part of these same followers in the light of eschatological times which have now begun. We see here the living Jesus giving his followers the concrete way of living *now*, the living sense of God's transcendence and love. God is perfect in love and has willed to be our Father. This theme is the very heart of the whole message of the Sermon on the Mount which Jesus has come to reveal to us; it now becomes the center of the new life of the followers of Jesus. Just as God loves all men, including sinners and those who are his enemies, and he continues to love them, so too, if men are to become his sons, they must do the same by imitating his love which is universal in scope. We are thus given a new morality of fraternal charity whose motivation is not simply eschatological, i.e., the judgment is near, but because we are sons of God, it follows that we must love as God loves. Thus the dynamic ethic of fraternal love is at the very heart of Christian morality and action.

The Sermon and its message can be called "the law of Christ." The Old Law with its many prescriptions which could all be accomplished without love in a ritualistic fashion has now been charged with a new attitude, a new dynamism. This ethic of Jesus has an unlimited horizon: Christians are to be perfect as God is perfect. This law of Christ is not a set of prescriptions as was the Old Law, but an orientation toward an imitation of God by loving our neighbor and our enemy, by indissoluble conjugal love, by complete sincerity and honesty in our relationship with other men. The only law is to love, an invitation to a new life lived according to the way in which God himself does things.

The drift of later Christian thought will be fundamentally the same, but it will shift from God to Christ as developed in the epistles of St. Paul. For instance:

> Therefore be imitators of God as beloved children. And walk in love, as Christ loved us and gave himself up for us, a fragrant offering and sacrifice to God (*Eph.* 5:1-2).

The imitation of God is here linked to the condition of sonship as its foundation. Man can imitate God on condition that he shares his life, since it is by God's love that a man is reborn into the life of the Spirit. This new life must be translated into loving action, into acts of love (cf. *Eph.* 4:32). This moral life of the Christian is therefore dynamic and active as shown in Christ who went to the cross for love of men. Our moral life must be a manifestation of love as was the life of Jesus.

Thus, in Matthew we have first of all a morality of hope which is an eschatological virtue for the future. It is both negative and positive. It is negative in that it sees that the world has no value in itself; Christians must spend their time preparing for his coming (watching, praying, being sober, etc.). But this is done in a positive fashion by doing God's will by and through fraternal charity. God is transcendent, it is true; yet the mystery of God's loving paternity is manifest to us in Christ's revelation. Christ asks us to be like God by imitating the Father's charity. The eschatological perspective, while not totally absent, is not a dominant theme in this chapter. Rather, it is a loving imitation of God *now* in our relationship with men here below. Indeed, we directly prepare for the last day by imitating God as his sons by and through fraternal charity.

St. Matthew uses the verb *agapan* for "love," not the Greek word *philein*, which means "to love in friendship," for it is impossible to have friendship with an enemy. Primarily *agapan* means to show respect and kindness. Even to enemies, we owe esteem, fair treatment and help in time of need. We truly show love toward them, because we wish them good things and do everything possible to see that they get them. As Jesus said, "You must love your enemies . . . pray for those who persecute you." Prayer is the greatest and most far reaching kindness, *agapan's* most expressive and always possible proof of our love. The example our Lord gives, shows that *agape* (love) is not a sentimental feeling, but the intention of doing and acting in a Christ-like manner. And further, in order to love those who are disagreeable or even dangerous, we can desire their good and truly love them only if we have a higher inspiration, and this inspiration is clearly a divine one. Therefore, in the Sermon on the Mount we have a fairly clear indication that to separate the two great commandments is an impossible task. To love both neighbor and enemy as God loves them, the Christian must be a son of God in the strictest sense of the word. Only those who have God for their Father and who love God are able to do what he does — that is, include all men in their charity and love.

III
GOOD WORKS OF CHRISTIANS AND
PURITY OF INTEREST
Mt. 6:1-18

The following section is treated separately here since it deals with the subjects of prayer and fasting, which are interrelated. It puts into practice the new spirit of love underlying the total Christian ethic here applied to the realities of almsgiving (vs. 2-4), prayer (vs. 5-6) and fasting (vs. 16-18). All of these verses, except 9-15, are found only in Matthew and seem to have retained the same form which they had in the oral tradition of early Christians. We shall examine each of them separately:

> Beware of practicing your piety before man in order to be seen by them; for then you will have no reward from your Father who is in heaven (*Mt.* 6:1).

This verse sums up the spirit of the whole chapter: all that we do is to be done out of a pure intention to love God and our brothers. It is in this sense that the justice of Christians must go beyond that of the Scribes and Pharisees (5:20). The difference here is not one of degree but of the *spirit* in which these realities are performed. Justice is a certain rectitude of life which was first given by God in and through the law. Jesus has now extended it to all things such as the "superrogatory" works of almsgiving and fasting.

We must also note the order in which these three realities are given to us. The first is almsgiving, and the second prayer. This would seem somewhat strange, but only until we have seen the reason for this. The basic format of the New Testament always places prayer after the texts on fraternal charity, for without the latter, the former is worthless. As an example, we may cite the texts of Luke in 10:38-42; 11:1-13 which have to do with prayer; but we see that they are immediately preceded by the story of the good Samaritan (10:29-37) which was the story of universal Christian charity *par excellence*. The present section of Matthew's gospel follows the same format as the rest of the New Testament in this regard.

The terminology which Jesus uses here to describe the acts of almsgiving and fasting is the same as that of the rabbis of his time. There is indeed some relationship between a good deed and a reward but with a special nuance. The reward (*misthon*) about which Jesus speaks is not in set formulas: if you do this you will receive this. It is God's answer and God's reward to the man who is generous. To such a man God gives the gift of the Kingdom, which is utterly out of proportion to anything man could possibly do. As an example we have almsgiving. The law simply instructed the people of God to pay what they owed. Anything more than this was not obligatory. It was the law of the "minimum" in order to escape injustice. The same regulation held true for other good works prescribed by the law. The law did not command the people to pray, but only to offer prescribed sacrifice at prescribed times. Fasting was not even part of the law. As such, a person could do all of these things in a purely ritualistic way (even for vainglory, to be esteemed by men) with no interior spirit. If such was the intention of the person, he will receive exactly what he seeks and nothing more. It will mean nothing to God and indeed be detrimental to the person himself, since he thereby renders himself a sort of hypocrite, since his external actions do not respond to the interior spirit. Christ demands first and foremost a purity of intention ("Blessed are the pure of heart," *Mt.* 5:8), since we must act for God alone. If we act for men — or for any other reason or person whatsoever — we are not acting for God, and it will count nothing with him. Thus the motive of prayer, almsgiving, etc., must be solely for the honor and glory of God.

> Thus, when you give alms, sound no trumpet before you, as the hypocrites do in the synagogues and in the streets, that they may be praised by men. Truly, I say to you, they have their reward. But when you give alms, do not let your left hand know what your right hand is doing, so that your alms may be secret; and your Father who sees in secret will reward you (*Mt.* 6:2-4).

Judaism placed a great importance on almsgiving at the time of Jesus. This was particularly brought out by the book of *Tobit* which was a book of edification for the Jews:

> Give alms from your possessions to all who live uprightly, and do not let your eye begrudge the gift when you make it. Do not turn your face away from any poor man, and the face of God will not be turned away from you. If you have many possessions, make your gift from them in proportion; if few, do not be afraid to give according to the little you have. So you will be laying up a good treasure for yourself against the day of necessity. For charity delivers from death and keeps you from entering the darkness; and for all who practice it, charity is an excellent offering in the presence of the Most High (*Tobit* 4:6-11).

The meaning behind this giving of alms was the biblical notion that sin was recognized to be the result of egoism whose cure was fraternal charity — concretely, a sharing of one's goods with the poor. The rabbinical literature of the time had it as a rule that at feasts and banquets there should be a sharing of that banquet with the poor and disadvantaged. Thus, in *Jn.* 13:27-30, when Judas left the banquet table to betray Jesus, the other disciples thought it quite natural that he was going out to share some of the banquet with the poor.

In our passage, Jesus uses the word "hypocrite." There is no equivalent of this in Hebrew or Aramaic but rather comes from the Greek meaning "actor" (one who puts on a mask). The word then came to mean a lawyer (one who pleads like an actor) and from there develops into the notion of one who is insincere or phony. The term which Christ uses here does not necessarily refer to the Pharisees alone, but could refer to a much wider audience. The modern equivalent for "to blow a trumpet" would be, I suppose, "to call in the press" in order to inform everyone of the good deed we are about to perform. Our deeds, however, should be done in secret so as to preserve our pure intention of doing them for God alone. We thereby seek to serve God alone, and this being so, he alone will be our reward. Christ says that "the right hand should not know what the left is doing." There is perhaps a more subtle form of temptation than blowing the trumpet before men. It is a certain form of self-centered smugness for a work well done. We are approving ourselves in our deeds, and this can be as destructive to a pure intention as the more gross temptation to sound our deeds before men. In both cases, these deeds are done "before men" (even if it be only ourselves). We must have a constant purification of intention or motive of why we perform the acts which we do. This is the meaning of not letting our left hand know what our right hand does.

Then follows the section on prayer (vs. 5-15):

And in praying do not heap up empty phrases as the Gentiles do; for they think that they will be heard for their many words. Do not be like them, for your Father knows what you need before you ask him. Pray then like this:

Our Father who art in heaven,
Hallowed be thy name.
Thy Kingdom come,
Thy will be done,
    On earth as it is in heaven.
Give us this day our daily bread;
And forgive us our debts,
    As we also have forgiven our debtors;
And lead us not into temptation,
    But deliver us from evil.

For if you forgive men their trespasses, your heavenly Father will also forgive you; but if you do not forgive men their trespasses, neither will your Father forgive your trepasses.

This exposé on prayer is one of the longest in the New Testament. The first thing which Christ does is to dispell what prayer is not (v. 5). Our prayer must be for God alone, not in order to be seen and praised by men. Men in ancient Israel frequently prayed at all times and in every place. (It can still be seen today in the Near East.) This is the oriental approach to prayer which was all pervasive and total. Thus a man who was holy could pray in the middle of a street or anywhere in the open. The obvious objection of Jesus is not to the place of prayer, but rather to the impurity of the intention of the one so praying, since he does it for vainglory. Our prayer must not only be external but it must proceed from a right intention.

If we pray for the esteem of men, then indeed that will be our exact reward and we need expect nothing from God. If our prayer has a right intention, then it is God who will give us our reward.

There is a slight discordance between verse 5 (it uses the second person plural) and verse 6 (which uses the second person singular). This verse (6) refers to II *Kings* 4:33: "So he (Elisha) went in and shut the door upon the two of them, and prayed to the Lord." The text of Matthew says that we must go to the most hidden room of the house (*tamieion*), indicating the principle that when we pray, we must have a purity of intention, that is, of pleasing only God and not man. Prayer is not even seen here as a means of obtaining things, but simply and purely to please God and for no other reason. This self-seeking (although not entirely absent by divine command: "give us this day our daily bread") can vitiate the very notion of prayer. We trust God completely in prayer knowing that *he* knows that we have need of all these things (cf. vs. 32-33). The essential value of prayer is the worship, service and love of God.

This verse concludes with the words "in secret," since God is everywhere; and he is not perceptible to our senses, but he sees us and answers our prayer. Thus prayer is a personal encounter with God wherever we are and wherever we pray. The wonder is that he listens and that he cares because he loves us. Thus the trust and confidence which must accompany every prayer.

One of the abuses of the pagans was much repetition of sayings, magical formulas and rituals which

were supposed to have some effect on God. Here it
is not a question of the purity of intention but of re-
jection. The word which Jesus uses here is *battalog-
esete* which means to speak rapidly or very badly.
The prayer of the pagans was mostly a lot of repeated
words and it was often found in many pagan rituals.
Christ tells us (vs. 7-8) that there is no need for his
followers to multiply many words in their prayers.
The reason is that their Father already knows their
every need and desire and they should trust and have
confidence in him: God *is* our Father; therefore he
will take care of us in his love. We must keep our
prayer simple, since this love of God follows us everywhere. The pagans considered God not as a loving
Father but as another great personage before whom
they stood and spoke much (flattery, praise, etc.) in
order to gain his favor for the personal needs of the
one who asks. That is why the pagan had to multiply
his prayers. The Christian knows that God is his
loving Father and he need not flatter him to gain his
good graces. He is already loved and known by God
— therefore he does not need to ask much, certainly
not in many words. Much as a child before his father
who is loved and taken care of by that father, so is the
Christian before God. He need use no great words, no
grand titles — only to ask in trusting simplicity. The
Christian can be very direct because he is already
intimate with his father. If, therefore, we truly believe
that God is our Father, we do not need many words
in addressing ourselves to him.

This leads directly to that prayer of intimacy
known as "The Our Father." A preliminary question

may be asked of this prayer: was it composed as such by Jesus or compiled together from the sayings of Jesus by the primitive Christian community? We do know that the community had a very strong sense of the Fatherhood of God. This is seen above all in the epistles of St. Paul. For instance, in *Rm.* 8:15-17:

> For you do not receive the spirit of slavery to fall back into fear, but you have received the Spirit of sonship. When we cry, "Abba, Father!" it is the Spirit himself bearing witness with our spirit that we are children of God and if children, then heirs, heirs of God and fellow heirs with Christ. . . .

This theme is present many times throughout the New Testament. There can be no doubt that this strong sense of the Fatherhood of God came directly from the spirit and teachings of Jesus, in his own attitude toward God and how he communicated this to us. Although we are not certain whether the "Our Father" was a direct prayer of Christ, it is beyond a doubt that it represents perfectly his spirit and attitude. It comes to us directly from the primitive Christian community which learned its attitudes and dynamism at the very feet of the Word Incarnate. This was the direct experience which Jesus had of God which is now preserved for us in the "Our Father."

This prayer is found here as well as in Luke, but situated differently in each account. Our present text of the "Our Father" in Matthew is found in the Sermon on the Mount, at the start of Christ's public ministry and within a context of purity of intention in prayer and in doing the works of mercy. Luke's account (11:1-5) is situated in a dialogue of Christian prayer. It is introduced by a brief historical section. Luke's account goes as follows: "He was praying in a certain place, and when he ceased, one of his disciples said to him, 'Lord, teach us to pray as John taught his disciples.'" The situation of this passage from Luke is the second part of Christ's life which leads toward his passion and death (the last twelve chapters of his gospel). This section describes Christ's long journey to Jerusalem in which the greater part of his activity was spent in the training of his disciples. Thus the context is concerned with prayer. Chapter 10:38-42 describes Mary as having chosen the "better part" because she listens in passive contemplation to the words of Jesus. It is this listening to God which is essential for true prayer. Jesus is once again at prayer, which was his normal activity at night (11:1), and we are told simply that it was just a certain place at a certain time. This immediately puts Christ in a different light from the average Israelite for whom time (feasts) and place (temple, synagogue, pilgrimages) were very important. Jesus, however, prays at all times and in all places and for all occasions. The activity of Jesus is never so great that he has no time to pray. Even in the midst of so important a work as evangelization, he takes time out to pray to God by himself.

After Christ has finished praying (and only then out of respect for the Master), the disciples come to him in order for him to teach them how to pray. They give as their comparison the fact that John the Baptist had taught his disciples how to pray. This passage must have been authentic, since otherwise this reference to the Baptist would have been eliminated, since John had little importance to later Christianity; nor would they have made Jesus do as John did, so as not to make Jesus look in some way inferior to John.

There is a difference here between the actions of Jesus and that of the prophets. Jesus is above all else a man of prayer and his followers must be the same type of men; they are associated with his prayer. The prophets never took the initiative but were called by God to do his bidding. When the people were converted to God in the Old Testament, they did so by becoming obedient to the law; here the followers of Jesus are not converted to the law but are taught to pray by the Lord himself. They address God in the knowledge that they are the sons of the heavenly Father. God gave his name (Yahweh, he who is) to the Israel of old and they could thus pray to him; in Jesus, God gives us his full revelation, that is, that he loves us and that he is our Father who cares for us. The knowledge which Jesus has of God is perfect, and that is why we can pray to God in this new and bold way. This passage from Luke (11:1) indicates that the disciples were well aware of this new knowledge and relationship which Jesus had to God. Just as his own way (*Mt.* Chapter 6) of living was the fulfillment of the law, so also is his prayer the fulfillment and the most perfect form of prayer. When he taught the disciples how to pray, he did not teach them a "technique," or the best time for prayer, but he taught them by *praying himself.* The followers of

Jesus, then, have as their essential function and activity to participate in the unique prayer of Jesus. They approach him to *ask* him how to pray. Prayer itself and the willingness to pray are both the grace of the Spirit.

The Our Father

The prayer which Jesus teaches by praying is that of the "Our Father" (*Mt.* 6:9-13). It is taught to the twelve (and is above all their prayer) and, through them, to the followers of Jesus. We shall see that many of the petitions in this prayer will be colored by the future apostolate and difficulties of the twelve, since certain of the petitions presuppose a mission on their part. The "Our Father" of Luke is shorter than that of St. Matthew. It runs as follows:

> Father, hallowed be thy name.
> Thy Kingdom come. Give us each our daily
> bread; and forgive us our sins, for we our-
> selves forgive everyone who is indebted to us;
> and lead us not into temptation (*Lk.* 11:2-4).

Luke's account omits the third petition of Matthew ("Thy will be done") as well as the last one ("Deliver us from evil").

The primitive origin of this prayer is attested to by the earliest Christian literature such as the *Didache*. This book says that Christians recited this prayer three times a day along with the doxology, "For thine is the Kingdom, and the power and the glory, forever.

Amen." Most Scripture scholars are agreed that this doxology was not an original part of the "Our Father," but it is very ancient and its theology flows from the prayer itself. None of the ancient manuscripts have an "amen" after this prayer.

The "Our Father" as given in Matthew's gospel is longer than Luke's and is divided into two main sections. The first group of petitions concerns God directly, and in them Jesus prays that the reign of God's glory be accomplished since the establishment of the Kingdom will manifest the holiness and glory of God. Thus:

"Our Father who art in heaven,
Hallowed be thy name.
Thy Kingdom come,
Thy will be done,
    On earth as it is in heaven.

The second section concerns the needs of the followers of Jesus with relationship to God. Thus:

Give us this day our daily bread;
And forgive us our debts,
As we also have forgiven our debtors;
And lead us not into temptation,
    But deliver us from evil.

Jesus spoke constantly of his Father in a very special sense. He almost always used the expression "His Father" to designate God. As a matter of fact, this was exactly the opposite of Old Testatment custom which avoided mentioning the name of God out of reverence. The Jews did not dare pronounce the name of *Yahweh* for fear of blashphemy. The word *Adonai* (Lord) was substituted for the name of God when pronounced. (This was later translated by the word *Kurios,* meaning the omnipotence of God over the whole earth.) Christ did not follow this tradition and used the word "Father" constantly to refer to God. Thus, when he referred to his own relationship with God, the term God as *The Father* was used; where the disciples were concerned; however, the expression was changed "your Father in heaven." The transcendence of God was thus safeguarded, and yet the personal relationship of followers of Jesus with God is also conserved. This concept of God as our Father goes beyond anything the Old Testament had given the Israelites.

In the concept of the fatherhood of God, two basic thoughts can be distinguished.

— It is the Father who gives life and being to his children. A child cannot even conceive of his own existence outside of his relationship with his father. The child simply *is* because of the total action of the father. The Hebrew way of naming children indicated this basic fact of existence. For instance, we read "Simon-bar-Jona" for Simon Peter, which means, literally, "Simon-son-of-Jona." The child is forever in a unique relationship with his father, who gave him existence. This was the basic reason why the father had authority over the child and indeed, in ancient civilization, absolute authority of life and death over the child. The child is secondary to the father because the child came *after* the father.

— Another essential characteristic of fatherhood for the Bible was the fact that the Father educates the child, and the task of raising a child was seen as a task of love. It is here that we find the most important element of fatherhood. Any animal can beget a young one, but only a *Father* can educate his child, that is, raise it in love. This is essentially and specifically human in the raising of children to maturity.

There was, however, a difference in paternity between the Greeks and Romans, on the one hand, and the Jews on the other. Among the former peoples the primary aspect of fatherhood was that of begetting children. For instance, in Aristotle's *Politics* (Book I, Chapter 7, line 1255^b) we read: "Zeus rules all men, because he is the father of men and of gods; the father rules like a king over his children whom he has begotten." This aspect of begetting children is emphasized among these people with the corresponding virtues of authority and obedience.

The Jews, however, hesitated to speak about a God who begot them — at least in the Greek and Roman sense of the word. This was to protect the profound transcendence of God; and the Jews feared to give the impression that there is any continuity of nature between God and man. He is the "totally other" who is not of this world and consequently could not really "beget" men.

Deut. 32:6 does use the word "father":

> Do you thus requite the Lord,
> You foolish and senseless people?
> Is not he your Father, who created you,
> who made you and established you?

Yet this terminology never became popular in Israel or in Jewish piety precisely because of the dangers named above. In the prayer life of the Jews represented for us above all in the Psalms, the name of God as Father never appears. He is called Lord, King, Shepherd, Leader, Rock, but never Father. In the whole Old Testament (outside of the above text of *Deuteronomy*) we find the word used only once in *Isaiah* 63:16, where God is called upon to remember his people as Father:

> For thou art our Father,
> Though Abraham does not know us and
> Israel does not acknowledge us;
> Thou, O Lord, art our Father,
> Our Redeemer from of old is thy name.

This text, however, is quite late in origin from after the return from the exile (538 B.C.). What the author is trying to suggest here is that God is *like* a father. In any case, the cry of Israel was never "Father" as one would say "Lord." The reason was the fear of the Jews of compromising God's transcendence. Nor does the Old Testament ever speak of men imitating God because of the dangers already mentioned.

Israel's idea of God's fatherhood was intimately related to the adoption of Israel by God in the covenant on Mt. Sinai. The following texts bring this out well: "Israel is my first born son" (*Ex.* 4:23). It was out of all the nations of the earth that God chose Israel for no other reason than that he wanted to, because of his love: "When Israel was a child, I loved him and out of Egypt I called my son" (*Hosea* 11:1). The term "child" indicates Israel's condition of slavery in Egypt. They were a despised people since they were slaves, and yet God loved them even before they had done any good whatever. It was because of this love that he gave them a vocation to bear his name:

Yet it was I who taught Ephraim to walk,
I took them up in my arms;
but they did not know that I healed them.
I led them with cords of compassion,
    with the bonds of love,
and I became to them as one who
eases the yoke on their jaws,
and I bent down to them and fed them
    (*Hosea* 11:3-4).

Thus the vocation of Israel was conceived as a child who is begotten and nourished because of the love of the Father. Israel at times did not realize that the Lord's commands were for its own good and were done out of love for no other reason.

Another image which *Hosea* used to express this relationship of love between God and Israel was that of an unfaithful spouse and her husband. In spite of the infidelity of Israel (adultery, idolatry), God did not abandon his people (*Hosea* 11:9). This prophetical tradition insists on God's love toward his people in his relationship to them. God is indeed the creator of Israel; yet the concept of "fatherhood" remains only one image among many others and never passed into the prayer of Israel (cf. *Isaiah* 64:8; *Jeremiah* 3:19; *Proverbs* 3:12).

When Jesus uses this term there is a great change change of perspective, since for Jesus, God is the Father in the strict sense of the word, to the extent that when we become disciples of Jesus we are the sons of God. This explains why he always refers to God as "Your Father who is in heaven."

This tradition of calling God "Father" was very ancient in the primitive Christian community. Even those Christians converted later who did not know Aramaic (the original language of Jesus) continued to use the Aramaic word for Father: "Abba." Thus the words of St. Paul: "For you did not receive the spirit of slavery to fall back into fear, but you have received the spirit of sonship. When we cry, 'Abba, Father!'" (*Rm.* 8:15). The word in Aramaic means "Father" but an emphasis on the tenderness of paternity, perhaps closer to our English "papa" or "daddy," as an expression of the greatest trust and confidence in God. He is someone who loves us absolutely no matter who we are and what condition we are in. There is no limit or condition to this love of God for men. Jesus showed this by his very life and death as a manifestation of God's absolute and unconditional love for men — above all for the despised and for sinners. This dimension of God's paternity was unheard of in either pagan or Jewish circles. This love of God for men is concretely expressed in the life, works and teachings of Jesus. In the teachings of Jesus, we have such parables as the prodigal son (*Lk.* 15:11-32) which showed God's tender mercy toward the sinner. By his actions, Christ showed this mercy of God to sinners by associating with public and notorious sinners.

We may conclude these observations concerning the fatherhood of God with a few remarks. One consequence of this new revelation of Jesus is a new awareness and certainty of God's personal and special love for each and every one of all men. If God cares for all creatures, how much more does he care for men? (*Mt.* 6:26). God watches over every one of them (*Mt.* 18:10-14). St. John (1:12) expands this notion of our divine sonship by emphasizing the power of God by which we are made sons by water and the Holy Spirit. St. Paul also develops this same theme and it becomes one of the major developments in his epistles. He says that we call upon God as Father because we have already become his sons and, if sons, then heirs of the Kingdom of God (*Rm.* 8:15). The Synoptic gospels are satisfied with giving us this essential teaching without developing it to any great degree.

There is another aspect of this teaching on the fatherhood of God which must be noted. The relationship of Jesus to God, his Father, is altogether extraordinary even in the texts of the Synoptic gospels. This relationship will be brought out further in the gospel of St. John and the epistles of St. Paul, but this special relationship of Jesus to God sets the whole tone for the "good news" of the gospel. There is no theological development of this "sonship" in Matthew, but then this was not at all necessary in a text which was primarily meant as a catechetical text for the first Christians. The only thing they had to know was that God was their Father and the way to become sons was to do what Jesus taught them to do.

But God is called "Our" Father in this prayer of Jesus (*Mt.* 6:9). Who is this "Our," since it is in the plural? Two answers are possible to this basic question:

— One is that it refers only to Jesus and his followers, since this seems to be the sense of the whole phrase. The early community was always conscious of the fact that it prayed with Jesus, and the reason its prayer was heard by God was that it prayed in union with Jesus even though we have no record in the gospels of Jesus praying with his disciples. When Jesus prays, he prays alone. We do have one example in the Passion (*Mt.* 26:38; *Mk.* 14:32; *Lk.* 22:40) where Christ asks the disciples to pray with him, but in each account he goes a little further along to pray by himself. This is to emphasize that the relationship of Jesus to his Father is unique and his prayer is beyond the possibilities of his disciples and can never be fully identified with human prayer. Here, when he teaches his disciples the "Our Father," he begins by saying: "When *you pray*" (*Lk.* 11:2). Thus Jesus does not identify himself with the "Our" in this prayer precisely because his relationship with God is so utterly unique. We read in the book of the *Didache* the following expression of these early Christians: "We give thanks to God, Our Father . . . through Jesus. . . ."

— The other opinion is that this "Our" in the prayer refers to all men, since God is the Father of all men. Most probably — in the opinion of the best Scripture scholars — the "Our" originally and historically referred to Christians alone, since it was only given to the disciples (even to the exclusion of the crowds of the Jews). Moreover, this becomes evident from the fact that the prayer contains a whole series of Christian themes (Kingdom come, forgiveness of each other, etc.) which can only be understood by those who have Christian faith. This prayer is an eschatological prayer of the Christian community and would be incomprehensible to those not of that faith.

On the other hand, it was later theologically developed to include all men, since God is the creator and provider of all men on earth. It is the will of God that all men be united to this Christian community of his son and in function of that, all men can call upon God as their Father.

"Who art in heaven"

The biblical notion of "heaven" and "earth" are not two localities but rather refer to the human and divine spheres. God is different from men; he is transcendent and in that sense is not "of this world." God is not man and man is not God. In order to express this form of difference, we have these two biblical notions of "heaven" and "earth." Indeed, we have here a sort of conveying of this basic idea of God's transcendence beyond this world. This transcendence of God, however, is the very measure of God's infinite love for the men of earth.

The first three petitions of the "Our Father" are petitions which have as their object God's *name, will* and *Kingdom*. The other three petitions which follow these are requests for the Christian's needs. These are very simple and direct, as befits a child who approaches his Father in love. Even the petitions themselves are different from the greedy requests of most people and particularly the pagans, who approached the gods for all forms of material goods. In the "Our Father" the Christian simply asks for bread, forgiveness and help in temptation.

Yet, it is the first three petitions which are the most important for the Christian. In them we petition God that *he* sanctify his name, that *he* realize his Kingdom on earth as well as his will. In the radical poverty which is ours, we can ask him to do only what he can do. Others have interpreted these petitions in a different fashion, particularly the Latin writers of the Church. They claimed that God's name is already sanctified and that the Kingdom has already arrived and God's will is already done in heaven. What remains is that we as Christians decide to realize his will, Kingdom and name on earth. Thus, these three petitions would not be petitions at all, but rather a commitment to the apostolate. Yet there is no reason to separate these two interpretations since the second is already implied in the first, and without the first, the second would cease to exist at all. I cannot pray God that his will be done, that his Kingdom come, without my willingness to fulfill my own role within God's plan of accomplishing this end. It is God who through us will accomplish his plan for men, for only God can do this. We ask God's grace in order to accomplish his will, and, as St. Augustine once put it, the ability to pray and the accomplishment of that prayer are both God's work. We can only say "yes" or "no" to God's plan for us.

Thus, the prayer of the "Our Father" begins not on a note of adoration, but filially, on the address of "Father" which betokens the whole new approach of Christians to God. They look to God for everything, depend upon him completely and trust him absolutely and love him and his will totally. It betokens as well the radical poverty of the Christian as given to us in the first beatitude: "Blessed are the poor in spirit."

"Hallowed be thy name"

A name in the Bible is important because it indicates a person in all of his power. The name of a person was indicative of who and what the person was. The name and the person could not be separated. A person's name indicated the kind of person he was or the function he had in life. Thus God renames Abram to Abraham (father of many nations, *Gen.* 17:5, and the renaming of Peter in *Mt.* 10:4; *Mk.* 3:16; *Lk.* 6:14). The name indicated the entire personality of the one named. The very reason we can use a name is that we at least have some familiarity with the person so named, that we know and understand that person, to a more or less degree. The parents would give the child a name as a sign of its destiny or, at least of what the parents wished the child to become. This was so with many personages of both the Old and New Testaments to whom God gave new names in order to indicate a new destiny or vocation.

In the Bible the name of God was considered in some way to carry God, to transmit God. That is why the Jews always avoided the use of the name of "Yahweh" in their prayers and readings of the Scripture and substituted a euphemism, "Kingdom of heaven," or another word ("the Lord"). The name of God implied knowledge of God plus a possibility of some communication or dialogue. This is true of men, and the Bible considered it true for man's relationship with God as well. In order to permit men to do so, God reveals his name to men, and he thereby establishes and creates the dialogue (*Ex.* 3:13-14). God manifests himself to man by giving man his name and so establishing a knowledge and communication between them. Israel not only "knew" the name of God but could now cry it out in prayer. It is the expression of the divine reality itself:

Behold the name of God comes from afar, burning with his anger, and in thick rising smoke; his lips are full of indignation and his tongue is like a devouring fire (*Isaiah* 30:27).

It is evident in this passage that "the name of Yahweh" means Yahweh himself as he manifests himself to men. Much like the term "glory of God," which means God's manifestation to men, so too with the name of God. Much more is present than is manifested to these men in the "name" or "glory" of God — but there is some form of communication present. God is present but he appears to men only to the extent that they can bear it. This is brought out in another passage from *Isaiah*: "So they shall fear the name of the Lord from the west, and his glory from the rising of the sun" (59:19). In this context, God's name and glory are used to indicate his power in defeating his enemies.

This name of God, continues the "Our Father," is sanctified (*hagiastheto*). The Greek word "hallowed" is proper to the Bible and cannot be found in pagan literature. It is the Greek translation of the Bible which purposely used variant Greek words to express and translate the Hebrew, since the Jews believe that the pagans were incapable of understanding the message of God.

We read in *Isaiah*: "But the Lord of hosts is exalted in justice, and the Holy God shows himself holy (*hitpahel*) in righteousness" (5:16).

The context here is one of judgment, and on that day the rich who enjoy themselves and their wealth today will be doomed on the day of judgment when all men will be humbled as God shows himself (Hebrew: "sanctify"). On that day only the glory of God will remain and be shown to men. He will re-establish justice, which has been destroyed by the greed and selfishness of the rich. This same sense is given in *Leviticus*: "Then Moses said to Aaron, 'This is what the Lord has said, I will show myself holy (*hitpahel*) among those who are near me, and before all the people I will be glorified'" (10:3). In the preceding verses of this chapter of *Leviticus*, God has shown his power in destroying sons of Aaron for doing what was not commanded. God speaks in this terrifying action. He thus shows that he is holy by this justice of chastisement. God's sanctity and holiness are manifested here in rejecting all impurity in his presence. We also have two passages from *Ezekiel,* the prophet:

> Thus says the Lord God:
> "Behold, I am against you, O Sidon, and I will manifest my glory in the midst of you. And they shall know that I am the Lord.
> When I execute judgments in her, and manifest my holiness in her" (28:22).

This is an oracle against Sidon, one of the oppressors of Israel. Even if Israel is presently defeated, this will not remain forever, for God will intervene in history and he will be glorified in that manifestation. The pagans think that God is impotent because he does not intervene to save his people, but he will intervene with all his power and he will show them who he is (Yahweh) as the powerful one.

> A second passage is taken from the same prophet:
> And I will vindicate the holiness of my great name, which has been profaned among the nations, and which you have profaned among them; and the nations will know that I am the Lord, says the Lord God, when through you I vindicate my holiness before their eyes (36:23).

The historical context here is the exile of Babylonia of 587 B.C. The prophets had often condemned the sins of Israel, but now this great punishment was upon them for all of their sins. Yet even at this tragic moment God does not abandon them, but gives them hope and solace through *Ezekiel* and the second part of the prophecy of *Isaiah*. As here shown, God loves Israel and God will lead Israel back to the promised land where they will be once again faithful to Yahweh. He will do this by punishing the enemies of Israel. The exile was willed by God because of the many sins of Israel, yet even in her fall the divine name has been profaned among the nations by the mocking attitude of these same nations who lead Israel into exile. Their God, conclude the pagans, must be a very weak God. It is Israel who is responsible for this profanation of God's holy name. But this is not God's last word. He will manifest his glory and glorify his name by bringing Israel back to the promised land. They will know that he is Yahweh. This will show his people his omnipotence in his dealings with them by washing away their sins and giving them a new spirit. He will replace their hearts of stone with hearts of flesh. God restores his name by his own work in manifesting his all-powerfulness (sanctity) by what he does for his people.

This petition of the "Our Father" is wholly a concept from the Old Testament. Christians ask for this eschatological event to be realized very soon by the power and intervention of God. This same motif is present in the third petition.

*   *   *

"Thy Kingdom Come, thy will be done on earth as it is in heaven"

This is perhaps the most important of these first three petitions since the other two are related to this one. This theme of the realization of the Kingdom was one of the most frequent in the preaching of Jesus. The will of God is the accomplishment of his Kingdom on earth in the last times. Since this is God's will, the Christian prays that it be accomplished. The eschatological nature of the passage is clearly indicated by the use of the subjunctive tense. We ask God to bring this about, but implicit within this petition, is our own willingness to participate in it.

The "will" of God as used here was hardly known among the pagan Greeks (they would have used the more intellectual word *boule*). Its origin means "a desire" even a "loving desire," since for the Jews every desire was desired with a sort of passion marked with strong emotion. There was little effort and less willingness in Semitic thought to separate the intellectual will from the affective desires which accompanied it. All willing is colored with affectivity — even for the will of God. As applied to God, the word "will" means the whole plan of God which he wants to realize. It is God's will which directs and orientates the whole history of Israel expressed in the law. This is seen in certain passages from the Old Testament:

> The Lord has established his throne in the heavens,
>   and his Kingdom rules over all.
> Bless the Lord, O you his angels,

> You mighty ones who do his word,
> hearkening to the voice of his word!
> Bless the Lord, all his hosts,
> his ministers that do his will (*Ps.* 103:19-21).

Here all of creation – angels as well as the rest of creation – is called upon to do God's will. All creation and the angels praise God precisely by doing his will. Only those who praise him can do his will and in praising they do his will. God's *will* is closely associated with his *word*, and by obeying his word we do his will. "Our God is in the heavens; he does whatever he pleases" (*Ps.* 115:3). Here we have the fact of divine transcendence (God is in heaven), but that God effects his will on earth as he pleases. He accomplishes his will in heaven and on earth.

> For I know that the Lord is great,
> and that our Lord is above all gods.
> Whatever the Lord pleases he does,
> in heaven and on earth ... (*Ps.* 135:5-6).

And, finally, we read in I *Maccabees* 3:60: "But as his will in heaven be, so he will do." Thus our petition of the "Our Father" asks God to accomplish the whole of his plan everywhere.

We may then conclude our discussion of the first three petitions of the "Our Father" by saying that they have an essential eschatological orientation. They comprise a realm of *hope* for the future at the final consummation of God's will at the *parousia,* or last coming of Christ. All things ultimately depend upon

God. The first petition comes from man's radical poverty since he knows that, of himself, he cannot do what he is asking God for. He can only beg God to accomplish what he asks for. It is a prayer of complete confidence, trust and love in the ability of God to do what we ask for. This faith and hope are themselves a part of the adoration of the Christian. But this hope is not only orientated to the future but also to the *now* in the measure that it can be realized here on earth in the "now." The Kingdom has begun on earth in an imperfect but true way, and so its effects must also be felt in witness in the "now" of its realization. As a conclusion to this section, let us quote the Jewish prayer called the "Kaddish." We are not certain whether this prayer antecedes Jesus or whether there is a Christian influence on the prayer. In any case, it expresses many of the themes of the "Our Father":

> May his great Name be kept magnificent and holy in the world which he has created according to his good pleasure. May he establish his Kingdom and may he make his Redemption appear; may he send his Messiah and may he buy back his people during your lifetime, during your days and during the days of the whole house of Israel, right away and soon ("Amen!" is said.).
>
> May the Name of the Holy One be blessed, praised, glorified, raised up, exalted, praised by word and song and raised on high; may he be praised above and higher than any other blessing, hymn, praise or consolation ever to be uttered! ("Amen!" is said.).

May your prayer be welcomed and may your petition be realized, along with the petition of the whole house of Israel, before our Father in heaven! May heaven produce a great peace, help, redemption, broadening, life satisfaction, salvation, consolation, deliverance, cure, buying-back, expansion and liberation for you and for us and for the community of the whole house of Israel, so that we may have life and peace " ("Amen!" is said.)

✿ ✿ ✿

The second group of petitions of the "Our Father" is longer than the first three petitions. The petitions are addressed to God, but their perspective is different since they now concern the needs and requests of Christians themselves.

"Give us this day our daily (epiousion) bread"

The gospel of Luke (11:3) has the following version: "Give us each day our daily (epiousion) bread." The Greek word which is translated "daily" (epiousion) is the same in both instances (which shows its primitiveness) and is found only once in profane Greek where it means "daily" or a day's work. The word is derived from the prefix epi which can be further derived from either of two verbs: ienai ("to go") or einai ("to be").

If this prefix is derived from the first verb, it would seem to mean "that which comes after" or a sort of surplus, or what will come tomorrow. Yet this would seem to contradict the other places in the same gospel where Christ tells us that we must not be solicitous for the morrow.

If this prefix comes from *einai* (to be) it would mean "what is after." Thus the disciples would be asking for "leftover bread," that is, only the minimum of what is necessary for survival. It can also mean simply the bread which we need for each day — as it is usually interpreted. In history, various authors interpreted this word in a more or less eucharistic sense, as if the Christians were here speaking of the eucharistic banquet which we know they celebrated from the earliest days. This meaning (eucharist) seems to be a later theological interpretation which has nothing to do with the text as recited by the first Christians.

Thus we may conclude that this word "daily" is not exactly a matter of chronology but simply an appeal for the bread which we must continuously have for our life. Nor does it mean that we are thereby dispensed from working for this bread in our human lives, but that we must have trust that, no matter what happens, God will give us the nourishment which we need. It is God who — above our every worry and solicitude — gives us our bread. We ask him only for what is necessary now, at this moment, not "worrying for the morrow." Once again, this shows us our radical poverty even in the search for earthly needs. Just as we would cease to exist if this bread were taken away, so it here becomes a *symbol* of our complete dependence upon God and his own good pleasure. We need God for *all* things not just for "spiritual" things, and it all becomes God's free gift to us. We may also conclude that the prayer implicitly approves of our asking for material necessities in a spirit of trust and confidence, but not in the spirit of materialism which seeks ever more, ever better. We ask only for what is absolutely necessary for our life and work and for nothing else — not comforts, which is against the whole spirit of this prayer. The disciples are called here to a life of voluntary poverty, for those who are neither sure of food or money. Much like the manna in the desert (*Ex.* 16:4-5) which was given to the chosen people only one day at a time and no more, so too with regard to our prayer here: we have no right to ask God for more than we need each day.

✿   ✿   ✿

"And forgive us our debts (opheilemata) as we have also forgiven our debtors."

Lk. 11:4 puts it: "And forgive us our sins (*hamartias*), for we ourselves forgive everyone who is indebted to us."

We immediately see that the direct object of the forgiving is different in Matthew (debts) from that in Luke (sins). The word "debts" which Matthew uses means "that which is due" but which has little significance. This is because Matthew envisioned a Christian community so strongly committed to Christ that their fault would only be small and insignificant.

Luke, on the contrary, uses the direct "sins" and is a stronger expression than that of Matthew. By the time Luke wrote it was a sad but real fact that Christians, too, could fall back into their former ways of sin.

In any case, this sense of sinfulness and of infidelity before the absolute holiness and sanctity of God is such that the Christian is always conscious of this separation and of his own impurity. As *Isaiah* (6:5) put it:

And I said: "Woe is me! For I am lost; for I am a man of unclean lips, and I dwell in the midst of a people of unclean lips; for my eyes have seen the King, the Lord of Host!"

Man's reaction before the holiness and totally "otherness" of God is one of awe. In the presence of God, man becomes conscious of his own sinfulness and infidelities. The closer a man comes to God, the more he realizes just how impure he is.

The second half of this petition is a living and filial appeal to God for divine pardon for our sins and infidelities. Yet this divine forgiveness is directly related to fraternal charity, that is, how we forgive one another. This theme is very popular in the New Testament. This can be seen in the immediate two verses after the "Our Father" (6:14-15) which act as a commentary on the prayer itself. That is, it has to do with the relationship between divine forgiveness and human forgiveness which, in context, are correlative one to the other. This can be seen from other sayings of Jesus later in Matthew's gospel.

Then Peter came up and said to him, "Lord, how often shall my brother sin against me, and I forgive him? As many as seven times?" Jesus said to him,

"I do not say to you seven times, but seventy times seven" (18:21-22).

Peter asks a rabbinical question on how many times ought we to forgive each other. Some rabbis claimed no more than seven times — which was considered generous. The answer of Jesus is absolutely unreasonable from a purely human point of view: there is no limit to our forgiveness of the brother. The following verses (23-35) give a whole parable to explicate this precise point. The parable contrasts the great and many sins of man vis-a-vis God (a "King") and the smallness of the sins which men commit against each other. If God forgives us so much, we must at least be willing to forgive the small things we have done to each other. As a matter of fact, it is clear from the parable that the divine forgiveness is in some way dependent upon this human forgiveness. Christ portrays this with great contrast of money (10,000 talents = $1,000,000 and 100 denarii = $20). This was impossible to repay from a human point of view. This forgiveness of our brother's debt must be real and authentic, not perfunctory or external. This is emphasized by v. 35 of this chapter: "So also my heavenly Father will do to everyone of you, if you do not forgive your brother from your heart" (*apo ton kardion,* cf. *Lk.* 7:41 for parallel passage).

Thus, pardoning those who have offended us is one of *the* most characteristic aspects of the Christian religion and the following of Christ. Love of enemies is its most extreme form (*Mt.* 5:44). God has forgiven us absolutely and has completely reconciled us to himself by the blood of his son. This was simply and purely because God loves man and for no other reason. Thus, how *infinite* the debt which man owes God. But God demands a double payment in this relationship of forgiveness. God first forgives us (*Mt.* 18:23-25), and *because* of this generous and gratuitous love of which we are the unworthy and undeserving objects, a change in our own moral conduct is *demanded* by this same God. We must forgive our brother the injury he has done to us "seventy times seven" or as often as it happens. We ask God to forgive us in the same measure and to the same extent that we forgive each other. The mutual and fraternal forgiveness becomes the necessary condition of our own pardon from God. We can see here how deeply the whole Christian ethic is based on the one requirement: fraternal love.

*　*　*

"And lead us not into temptation,
But deliver us from evil" (*Mt.* 6:13, cf. Lk. 11:4)

We ask God not to "lead" us (*eisenegkes*) into temptation, and the Greek word used is the same in Matthew and Luke. Its original meaning is "do not let us fall," "do not let us succumb to." The word is used in other places in the New Testament as well. Luke uses it in two other places in his gospel:

And behold, men were bringing on a bed a man who was paralyzed, and they sought to bring him in (*eisenegkein*) and lay him before Jesus, but finding no way to bring him in (*eisenegkosin*), because of the crowd, they went up on the roof and let him down . . . (5:18-19).

And again:

And when they bring you (*eispherosin*) before the synagogues and the rulers and the authorities, do not be anxious how and what you are to answer or you are to say (12:11).

We have other passages as well:

For you bring (*eisphereis*) some strange things to our ears (*Acts* 17:20)

For we brought (*eisenegkamen*) nothing into the world, and we cannot take anything out (*exenegkein*) of the world (I Tim. 6:7).

For the bodies of these animals whose blood is brought into (*eispheretai*) the sanctuary by the high priest as a sacrifice for sin are burned outside the camp (*Hebrews* 13:11).

From all these passages we may conclude that this world means to "introduce" or "to make enter." What we are asking God in this petition is that he not make us enter into temptation.

But what is this "temptation"? We have a possibility of two meanings. The first comes from the earliest books of the Old Testament where the word refers to a trial which can be overcome in either of two ways: absolute confidence and trust in God or treason to God (cf. *Ex.* 20:20; *Deut.* 8:2; *Judges* 2:22). The life of faith, then, is necessarily a trial on earth, and we will be tempted to betray God throughout this life or throughout this trial. This interpretation is not completely satisfactory since, if life is a trial, we cannot very well ask God to relieve us of this trial whereby and wherein we prove our fidelity to him. We can only grow in this trial. Nor can we say that God actively leads men into trials and temptations.

Therefore, a second meaning can be given to this word "temptation" which comes from the time of the later prophets (Daniel in particular). During this period "temptation" meant a "great trial" which will come at the end of time when the Lord comes, or on the last day. At that black hour the powers of the world shall seem to overcome men and events, whereupon the eschatological trial will be upon us. Jesus used this word precisely in such an eschatological context. Thus: "Take heed that no one leads you astray (*planese*)" (*Mt.* 24:3-44). In the context, the disciples ask Christ what will be the signs of the last day (*parousia*). Christ then outlines the signs which will accompany this period, and the great "temptation" of Christians will be that the world will seem to overcome and the triumph of evil will seemingly be complete. Christians must not succumb to that "great" temptation, but persevere in fraternal love to the very end. Even the charity of many Christians will grow cold (v. 12). There will be the trials and tribulations in the times to come and it will be difficult to hold on to Christian charity. The antidote during these days will be prayer (v. 20). The only recourse in the face of this terrible trial is prayer to God that we not fail in our commitment. We pray in the "Our Father" that God not abandon us during those terrible days.

This same theme can be observed in the passion of Christ: "And when he came to the place (Mount of Olives) he said to them: 'Pray that you may not enter into temptation'" (*Lk* 22:40). (Christ uses the same word for temptation [*peirasmon*] as does the "Our Father.") Thus, prayer binds us to God as a guarantee against our fall or infidelity during a time of trial. In the "Our Father" we ask God that we be not menaced by the final (eschatological) trial or for God to restrict its force upon us; and although this petition refers primarily to the trials before the *parousia*, by amplification, it is also directed toward every temptation to which we are subjected during the whole period of life which, in a sense, is also part of our eschatological event. The symbols of this eschatological trial are given to us in Mt. 24:1-36 and above all in *Revelation*. These symbols suggest the real meaning of the present time in the Christian community wherein the Christian is continuously tried in his faith and fidelity. His only recourse in and throughout this period of trial (that is, throughout life) can only be confident prayer to the Father who can give the grace and strength to overcome these trials.

Thus Christians must be continuously vigilant and always men of prayer before the *parousia*, or Christ's second coming. In all of this, Christ is our model who continuously prayed, but particularly before the great events of his life (before his public life, before choosing his disciples, before his passion and even on the cross itself). Our only hope is to recognize our weakness and complete poverty and have *absolute* recourse to God, our Father.

✿　✿　✿

"But deliver us from evil"

The Greek word for "deliver" (*hrusomai*) literally means to free from captivity or from a net. In the Old Testament it is used in the context of the Lord coming to save his people from danger: "For thou hast delivered me from every trouble, and my eye has looked in triumph on my enemies" (*Ps.* 54:7).

The word "evil" can either refer to the neuter and, as such, to a state of being evil; or to the masculine, in which it would refer to the Devil. Either of these two meanings is possible. Parallel passage where this word is used can perhaps give us a better idea of its use.

Many parables speak of "evil" men but, then, being parables, they might refer symbolically to a deeper and more profound evil reality.

II *Timothy* 4:18 speaks of evil works: "The Lord will rescue me from every evil work and save me for his heavenly Kingdom." (*onerou* = evil work, and *rusetai* = rescue, deliver, which are the same words used by Matthew in this petition of the "Our Father.") However, the "evil work" may be understood as the "evil work of the evil one or devil."

Mt. 4:1-11 itself speaks of a devil or "Satan"

and seems to indicate a person who seeks to bring about man's destruction. Yet, here also, we are not certain whether what is envisioned is an evil person called "devil" or a symbol of the deeper reality of evil in the hearts of men.

Let us conclude by saying that this final petition asks God that we be not handed over to this adversary called "evil" or "the evil one" from which we have been redeemed by Christ. Once again, it is only God who can give us the strength for this deliverance.

✻ ✻ ✻

Concluding advice: Fasting (Mt. 6:16-18)

We now return to a style that was characteristic of the early saying of this chapter concerning almsgiving and prayer:

> And when you fast, do not dismay, like the hypo-crites, for they disfigure their faces that their fast-ing may be seen by men. Truly I say to you, they have their reward. But when you fast, anoint your head and wash your face, that your fasting may not be seen by men but by your Father who is in secret; and your Father who sees in secret will reward you.

We must remember that fasting among the Jews was a strong Old Testament custom of penance. Its origin was probably in that mourning where everyone's sadness at the loss of a loved one is expressed by a complete refusal of food. When the Jews fasted, it became evident to all those around him, since it was accompanied by external ritual ascetical practices. Thus, the clothing was supposed to be unclean and disheveled, and he did not wash himself. (Men even shaved themselves, beard and head, in order to deprive themselves of the beauty of these masculine traits.) This would continue for about two days a week, on which days the pious Jew would eat nothing.

Jesus had a nuanced position in regard to fasting. He does not reject it. (He practices it at times himself [cf. *Mt.* 4:1], but does not stress it as much as did John the Baptist.) He enjoins the disciples to do what the law prescribed but no more (*Mt.* 9:14-18). His emphasis was always on the doing of the works of justice and mercy (the whole Sermon on the Mount is geared to precisely this) for the sake of God alone and not for the esteem of men. Thus, as we have said, what Christ inculcates is not that these works are to be done away with, but that we do them with a purity of intention in order to please God alone. In fasting, the Christian's intention is to be for God alone as an act of submission to him and dependence upon him alone.

IV
CHRISTIAN WISDOM

The remaining counsels of the Sermon on the Mount are somewhat different from the ones which we have thus far seen in that the following are less strictly inter-connected.

Vs. 19-20 are verses which have as their purpose to introduce the rest of the Sermon. They have to do with a treasure as a precious object which has become the preoccupation of the whole life of a person who finds it; so much so that he concentrates his whole life on its search and retention:

> Do not lay up for yourselves treasures on earth, where moth and rust consume and where thieves break in and steal, but lay up for yourselves treasures in heaven, where neither moth nor rust consumes and where thieves do not break in and steal. For where your treasure is, there will your heart be also.

There are two different types of treasure described for us in the text and they are opposed to each other:

– The one treasure is on earth (money). Such

treasure can be attacked and destroyed by other earthly things such as thieves and moths (cf. *Malachi* 3:11). In those days, this was a comparatively simple thing to do, since the homes were made of mud and wood. Earthly things can and will destroy earthly treasure.

— The second form of treasure is heavenly, whose values are with God who will keep them safe from all loss or corrosion. This is indeed a judgment against money (cf. *Mt.* 6:24); however, it is 'not a condemnation of material things but, rather, of a *spirit* of greed and selfishness that often, in fact, accompanies an abundance of material goods. Christians are to have money, and the New Testament many times refers to this fact; yet, they were to use these material goods for the service and promotion of fraternal charity. Wealth and money were not central preoccupations in their lives since this central place was filled by a love of God and love of the brothers.

Lk. 12:33-34 has a parallel passage but with an emphasis on the fact that no one can have two treasures to which he can be completely dedicated. Luke, who is, as we know, the evangelist of material poverty, emphasizes that in order for the Christian to have the treasure of heaven, he must sell his possessions and give alms, which will insure him of that heavenly treasure:

Sell your possessions, and give alms, provide yourselves with purses that do not grow old, with a treasure in the heavens that does not fail, where no thief approaches and no moth destroys. For where your treasure is, there will your heart be also.

Matthew continues his sayings of Jesus and this time a metaphor is used concerning a sound or healthy eye:

The eye is the lamp of the body. So, if your eye is sound, your whole body will be full of light; but if your eye is not sound, your whole body will be full of darkness. If then the light in you is darkness, how great is the darkness (6:22).

And the parallel passage of Luke's gospel (11:34-36):

Your eye is the lamp of your body; when your eye is sound, your whole body is full of light; but when it is not sound, your body is full of darkness. Therefore be careful lest the light in you be darkness. If your whole body is full of light, having no part dark, it will be wholly bright, as when a lamp with its rays gives you light.

The imagery is clear here: the eye is like the lamp for the body and by it the whole body is enlightened. If it is "simple" (that is, healthy) the whole body will be in light; but if it is diseased or blinded, then the whole body is without light. This imagery is intended to point out the moral connotations of the way we are to use our bodies and our eyes. This can also be seen as a form of parable in which the "body" stands for the soul and the "eye" for a form of spiritual insight. In this case, the basic idea would be that the light of our soul is our conscience. For a more profound explanation, we must investigate this imagery as it appears in the texts of the Bible.

The image of the "bad eye" is used in the Bible to convey bad moral dispositions (cf. *Mt.* 20:15). A person who has a "bad eye" is filled with jealousy and envy. He dares to say nothing but he is furious by means of a powerful look.

The "simple" eye also has moral considerations. There are two ways of explaining this concept of "simple" in the New Testament:

1. The word often means "generous" or the opposite of one who is envious or avaricious. Thus *Rm.* 12:8 speaks of a man who gives in simplicity: "He who exorts, in his exortation; he who contributes in generosity (*haploteti*)." The text refers to deacons who by their very office were to share the goods of the community with the poor. Thus their manner of giving must be generous and without calculation.

In another epistle, St. Paul says much the same thing. "For in a severe test of affliction, their abundance of joy and their extreme poverty have overflowed in a wealth of generosity (*haplotetos*) on their part" (II *Cor.* 8:2). The context is the collection which Paul was gathering for the poor Christians at Jerusalem. He gives them the example of the Macedonians who, in spite of their great trials and poverty, still managed to give in their generosity.

We have the same word used in the same sense in II *Cor.* 9:11-13:

> You will be enriched in every way for great generosity (*haploteta*) which through us will produce

thanksgiving to God.... Under the test of this service, you will glorify God by your obedience in acknowledging the gospel of Christ, and by the generosity (*haploteti*) of your contribution for them and for all others.

Finally St. James uses this word in the sense of generosity of a person who gives munificently and who is thus called "simple": "If any of you lacks wisdom, let him ask God who gives to all men generously (*haplos*) and without reproaching, and it will be given to him" (*James* 1:5). Thus, it is God who gives generously without counting the cost. The Christian must imitate God who gives without calculation or "what's in it for me" attitude.

If we accept this meaning of "simple" as denoting generosity, then *Mt.* 6:22-23 makes much sense, since the text is both preceded and followed by passages which oppose the goods of this world with the goods of the heavenly Kingdom. In order to choose between the two the Christian must have a "sound" or a "good" eye, which is characterized by a generous Christian commitment. If we give our all to the Kingdom, our whole being will be full of light as well as a source of light for others. If we give with a "bad eye," it is out of stinginess and we are dark. If, therefore, the Christian who is supposed to be light is in reality darkness, how great and complete will be the darkness of the world.

2. Other scholars claim that the meaning of the word "simple" (*haplous*) can be found only in the Old Testament where it means "the requirements for

total giving." Thus the Greek word for "simple" given to us in the Greek translation of the Hebrew Bible means and indicates the integrity of a person's generosity. It is a generosity without reserve found in every aspect of a man's life. It is not just generosity in giving alms, but a commitment of one's whole life. If the eye is "simple," it is that the man has a complete purity of intention in everything he does (he is not self-serving). You cannot serve the Christian commitment in a half-hearted way:

> I know, my God, that thou triest the heart, and hast pleasure in uprightness (*haplous*); in the uprightness (*haplous*) of my heart. I have freely offered all these things, and now I have seen thy people, who are present here, offering freely and generously to thee (I *Chronicles* 29:17).

The prayer here is addressed to Yahweh by Daniel the Prophet. He speaks of the people's generosity which has made the building possible. The intention of the people was pure and free. God knows this since nothing can remain hidden from God, even if others will never know it. It is pleasing to God that we give him our hearts freely and fully ("in the uprightness of heart"). The prayer here praises the completely pure intention of the heart (cf. *Wisdom* 1:1 and II *Samuel* 15:11). Generosity in this biblical sense of the word would only be one wider aspect of the original purity of intention ("blessed are the pure of of heart"). Thus our text (*Mt.* 6:22), when it speaks of a "simple eye," is not just speaking of a generosity of giving alms, but a wider purity of intention – which fits in well with the whole of chapter 6. Thus – as with prayer, fasting and almsgiving – it is the purity of intention which is all important. We cannot do any of these things by a partial commitment to man and a partial commitment to God. Our lives must be wholly generous and committed, else we become a scandal to the whole world; we are darkness.

Again Matthew comes back to the antithesis between God and mammon (money) as one of love and hate (that is, to love less). Once again, we cannot have two values to which we are totally and fully committed; one or the other will, of necessity, have to be subordinated to the other. To think otherwise is to live a life of illusion. There can be no other absolute value than God; if there is, then God is not the absolute first in our lives but is replaced by mammon (an Aramaic word meaning all forms of earthly riches):

> No one can serve two masters; for either he will hate the one and love the other, or he will be devoted to the one and despise the other. You cannot serve God and mammon (*Mt.* 6:24; cf. *Lk.* 16:13).

Thus, once again, we have here the absolute primacy of God in the lives of Christians which is central throughout the Sermon on the Mount. All other things must find their meaning in the light of this central reality. Everything else (mammon) is only instrumental at arriving at this supreme end (God, love of the brother).

The 6th chapter of Matthew ends with a description of this Christian attitude and center of his life — God and his Kingdom:

> Therefore I tell you, do not be anxious about your life, what you shall eat or what you shall drink, nor about your body, what you shall put on. Is not life more than food, and the body more than clothing? Look at the birds of the air. They neither sow nor reap nor gather into barns, and yet your heavenly Father feeds them. Are you not of more value than they? And which of you by being anxious can add one cubit to his span of life? And why are you anxious about clothing? Consider the lilies of the field, how they grow; they neither toil nor spin; yet I tell you, even Solomon in all his glory was not arrayed like one of these. But if God so clothes the grass of the field, which today is alive and tomorrow is thrown into the oven, will he not much more clothe you, O men of little faith? Therefore do not be anxious, saying, "What shall we eat," or "what shall we drink" or "what shall we wear?" For the gentiles seek all these things; and your heavenly Father knows that you need them all. But seek first his Kingdom and his justice, and all these things shall be yours as well (*Mt.* 6:25-33; cf. *Lk.* 12:22-31).

The text itself is self explanatory and needs little commentary. The basic theme here is one of anxiety and worry. The natural reaction of human beings is to say that all that has preceded in the Sermon on the

Mount is well and good but "let's be realistic." This basically human attitude, says Jesus, is not and cannot be enough for the Christian. His life is more valuable than food, drink and clothing. The birds have everything necessary to live (taken care of by God) and they do not work and toil. They are not anxious or worried. Thus the thought of Jesus reaches a climax in vs. 32-33: the reason we worry is that we have so little confidence in God and our worries are just like the pagans; and if we are Christians, what makes us any better than pagans when they worry about these earthly things? For the pagans, the search for material things is the totality of their lives. Jesus invites his followers to have an entirely new attitude. They must recognize God as their Father and put their *total* trust in him. God will not abandon his children. We must do our part but we must not be dominated by worry about these things. We must be completely dominated by a great sense of God's paternity with regard to ourselves, and he will not abandon us in all of our needs.

V

DISUNIFIED SAYINGS OF JESUS

This chapter concludes the Sermon on the Mount, but it is characterized by a series of disunified sayings of Jesus. We may note them together while adding the corresponding passages from the gospel of Luke:

	Matthew	Luke
Judgment of the Neighbor	7:1-5	6:37-38; 41-42
Short maxim—Holy things	7:6	— — —
Prayer	7:7-11	11:9-13
The Golden Rule	7:12	6:31
Narrow road and the gate	7:13-14	13:23-24
Against false prophets	7:15-21	6:43-46
Against self-deception	7:22-23	13:26-27
Active and practical fidelity	7:24-27	6:41-49

Judgment of the Neighbor (*Mt.* 7:1-5):

Judge not, that you be not judged. For with the judgment you pronounce you will be judged, and the measure you give will be the measure you get. Why do you see the speck that is in your brother's eye, but do not notice the log that is in your own eye? Or how can you say to your brother, "Let me take the speck out of your eye" when there is a log in your own eye? You hypocrite, first take the log out of your own eye, and then you will see clearly to take the speck out of your brother's eye.

The expression used here, "Do not judge," does not refer to the legal system of the courts. It refers directly to the judgments we form of other people, particularly of their motives; and in this case — as is often in the New Testament — the word "judgment" means "condemnation." The attitude we have toward others will be the attitude which God will have for us in a sort of reciprocity. We can, at any time, know God's attitude toward us by the attitude we have toward others.

The gospel of Luke develops this theme of reciprocity even more forcefully:

Judge not, and you will not be judged; condemn not and you will not be condemned; forgive and you will be forgiven; give, and it will be given to you. . . . For the measure you give will be the measure you get back (6:37-38).

Luke insists that what binds us together is always and everywhere *fraternal charity;* charity does not condemn but forgives. We are often struck by the seemingly evil intentions of others, and it demands the greatest fraternal charity to see this evil and yet to pardon it anyway. When we pardon real evil in others, it is fraternal charity which has become dominant in our lives, and it is only when our lives are so ruled that God forgives us. We indeed must judge the actions of others — this is inevitable, especially when they do us evil — but we must not condemn them but pardon and love them, even in spite of the real wrong which they have done to us. In any case, even before we do this, we must examine ourselves first to see that we often do the same things. How can we rebuke others for what we ourselves do, and if we do judge, we must do so humbly and with forgiveness.

The next maxim has to do with "holy things": "Do not give dogs what is holy; and do not throw your pearls before swine, lest they trample them underfoot and turn to attack you" (*Mt.* 7:6).

Christ here gives us a parable, since dogs and swine were considered impure by the Jews. Swine were impure due to the fact they were often used as animals of sacrifice among the pagan Canaanites and, therefore, the Jews were forbidden to eat pork. It could be that this image is used to describe the pagans and sinners. To these, we are forbidden to give "what is holy" (*hagion*). This term was often used to describe the sanctuary of the temple or "Holy Place" in the temple of Solomon. The *Didache* later applied this verse of Matthew to the Eucharist. Most probably what Matthew is referring to is the doctrine of the Kingdom which Christ is giving his followers.

The reference to the "pearls" can be compared with *Mt.* 13:45-50 which is the parable about the merchant who is searching for precious pearls, which, when he finds them, sells all he has and buys that pearl (the Kingdom). Christ would be saying here that we are not to give the Kingdom to our enemies (dogs). St.

Paul in *Philip* 3:2 uses the term "dog" to describe the adversaries of Christianity. Again, II *Peter* 2:22 uses the same word to describe bad Christians. What we can say is that this saying of Jesus is a form of general advice given to the Apostles before they are sent forth as missionaries. They are to be as "simple as doves and as wise as serpents." They are not to confuse naiveté with simplicity, and they must be circumspect at all times.

This is followed by the theme of constancy and fidelity in prayer — a theme that we have seen above (*Mt.* 6:13):

> Ask, and it will be given to you; seek and you will find; knock and it will be opened to you. For everyone who asks receives, and he who seeks finds, and to him who knocks it will be opened. Or what man of you, if his son asks him for a loaf, will give him a stone? Or if he asks for a fish, will give him a serpent? If you, then, who are evil, know how to give good gifts to your children, how much more will your Father who is in heaven give good things to those who ask him? (*Mt.* 7:7-11)

Jesus is speaking here not of the prayer of adoration (cf. *Mt.* 6:5-8) but of the prayer for petition of needed goods. Jesus commands us to ask with confidence and certitude that we will receive what we ask for, and this because of the *fatherhood* of God. We are conscious of being his sons and therefore should approach God without fear or hesitation.

This prayer is not sporadic or said only when we are in need. We must not be discouraged, but *constantly* ask in patience. On the one hand, God is our Father and cannot refuse our request — of this we are confident. That is why we must ask constantly, never ceasing out of discouragement. In order to illustrate this point, Christ takes examples from the daily lives of his listeners (stone, serpent); and if human fathers with all their ignorance and evil give good things to their children, how much more will God, our Father, do for us? Jesus conveys the essential message again: God is very serious and he loves man, which is the whole message of the Sermon on the Mount.

Christ then gives us the "Golden Rule" (*Mt.* 7:12; *Lk.* 6:31): "So whatever you wish that men would do to you, do so to them, for this is the law and the prophets." Christ here asks us to change our whole perspective from that of our natural inclinations. Naturally speaking, we are inclined to view others in terms of their duties toward us. Christ asks us here to go outside of ourselves *first* to others and be concerned first about their welfare. Moreover, Matthew uses the the word *anthropoi* ("men") in order to indicate that Christ is not just referring to the Christian community but to all men; we are to reach out to all men. The reason for this is quite evident from the Sermon on the Mount: charity knows no bounds, not even that of the Christian community.

Christ now goes on to discuss the difficulty in attaining salvation (*Mt.* 7:13-14):

Enter by the narrow gate; for the gate is wide and the way is easy, that leads to destruction, and those who enter by it are many; for the gate is narrow and the way is hard, that leads to life, and those who find it are few.

Jesus here distinguishes two routes, two ways of walking and of seeing life. The contrast is with the "wide" road (that is, very easy to follow) and with the narrow road (a road which is very difficult to follow). The imagery is very familiar not only to semitic thought, but to Greek thought as well (cf. *Jeremiah* 21:8; *Proverbs* 28:6-10; *Ps.* 118). The idea of two paths, one which leads to life and the other to death, is classical. The only difference between these traditional images and Christ's words here is that Christ says that the wide and easy path to perdition is found without searching for it, whereas the road that leads to life: those who walk in the law of the Lord must be conscious of what they are doing and be responsible for it. It is not "natural" to follow Christ's path, but must be a positive choice on the part of the person who follows it. That is why there are few who find it and follow it. The basic message here is a consciousness on the part of Christ and the community that the vast majority of men will not respond to the message of Christ, since it is so difficult and goes against the natural inclinations of men. Men must reflect on the meaning of their lives, and this is exactly what Christ here is asking us to do. In fact, most men just drift along with no meaning or direction to their lives. The message is indeed addressed to *all* men (sinners, poor, pagans, rich, the suffering), but each and every person must make a personal choice and decision. This passage is not a form of "predestination" but a simple observation that, although all men are called to this message, the great majority of men will not respond to it. The message of Jesus demands an active response from every man who chooses Christ.

Christ now gives us a warning concerning false prophets:

> Beware of false prophets, who come to you in sheeps' clothing but inwardly are ravenous wolves. You know them by their fruits. Are grapes gathered from thorns or figs from thistles? So, every sound tree bears good fruit, but the bad tree bears evil fruits. A sound tree cannot bear evil fruit, nor can a bad tree bear good fruit. Every tree that does not bear good fruit is cut down and thrown into the fire. Thus you will know them by their fruits (*Mt.* 7:15-20; cf. *Lk.* 6:42-45).

Many false prophets appeared in the Old Testament, and it was always a problem to be able to distinguish the good from the evil, the true from the false. Christ tells us that the only valid criteria here are his actions.

The false prophet seeks his own advantage, seeking to gain not obedience to God's word, but rather money, prestige, favor, etc. He attempts to please his listeners, to flatter those who listen to him. The classical false prophets were those in the Old Testament gathered around the king who would tell him exactly what he wanted to hear. Whatever the king wanted was construed by these prophets as the "will of God." Thus the false prophet becomes disturbed in the presence of a true prophet: "O seer, go, flee away to the land of Judah, and eat bread there, and prophesy there; but never again prophesy at Bethel, for it is the King's sanctuary" (*Amos* 7:12). The reason for this was that Amos, the true prophet, prophesized the destruction of the kingdom, and this the king did not wish to hear (7:17).

The true prophet is quick to point out God's will even when it will cost him dearly from a personal point of view, even when it goes against his own personal view (Jeremiah).

This whole passage of Matthew should be read in light of *Mt.* 24:4,5,24,45 and *Mk.* 13:5-6,22,34, where the eschatological perspective is evident:

> And Jesus answered them, "Take heed that no one leads you astray. For many will come in my name, saying, 'I am the Christ,' and they will lead many astray" (vs. 4-5).
> For false Christs and false prophets will arise and show great signs and wonders, so as to lead astray, if possible, even the elect (v. 24).
> Who then is the faithful and wise servant, whom the master has set over his household, to give them their food at the proper time? (v. 35)

It was evident that when these texts were written Christ was gone from the midst of the Christian community with the corresponding danger of false prophets rising up in the community and speaking against the received tradition of Christ in order to please men. The community gives us the distinguishing characteristics of these false prophets who would seduce others by their false ideas. We are told to watch their works and not their words (in the words of Lenin, "Watch their hands not their mouths"). Only the quality of a man's life will reveal who he is and will be a guarantee of his message. Thus a continuation of the description of the true Christian:

> Not everyone who says to me, "Lord, Lord" shall enter the Kingdom of heaven, but he who does the will of my Father who is in heaven. On that day, many will say to me, "Lord, Lord, did we not prophesy in your name, and cast out demons in your name?" And then will I declare to them, "I never knew you; depart from me, you evildoers" (*Mt.* 7:21-23; cf. *Lk.* 6:46).

Those who flatter their listeners are not the ones who will enter into heaven — even in spite of works and signs which they might do, but only those who do God's will (the whole Sermon on the Mount).

CONCLUSION

The Sermon on the Mount is a short resumé of the new spirit and the new religion of those who would follow Christ. Christ goes beyond the ancient law of the Jews by insisting that this new mode of life has as its essential characteristic and distinguishing mark the love of God and fraternal charity, which are the whole basis of the Christian faith. Even while insisting on the transcendence of God ("Your Father who is in heaven"), Christ reveals that he also cares for men, that he loves them far more than they can ever imagine. In reality, God is their father and they are his sons. God is beyond us, but he also touches us at our deepest level. This is the will of God for us as revealed by him who knows this will perfectly: Christ. Thus in whatever the followers of Jesus do, they must do it with the purest intention of love of God and love of neighbor. St. Paul gives us a beautiful summary of the spirit of the whole Sermon on the Mount:

Owe no one anything, except to love one another; for he who loves his neighbor has fulfilled the law.

The Commandments, "You shall not commit adultery, You shall not steal, You shall not kill, You shall not covet," and any other commandment, are summed up in this sentence, "You shall love your neighbor as yourself." Love does no wrong to a neighbor; therefore love is the fulfillment of the law (*Rm.* 13:8-10).

The whole Sermon on the Mount is the person of Jesus who is the love of the Father for men, teaching men that they are sons of the Father and therefore radically brothers. The dynamic newness of this new religion is its insistence on the central basis of fraternal charity.